THE EVACUATION OF SINGAPORE TO THE PRISON CAMPS OF SUMATRA

In memory of all who suffered at Muntok, Bangka Island, in Palembang and Belalau prison camps in Sumatra between 1942 and 1945, and the many evacuees from Singapore who did not reach land, and for their families.

And to our friend, the late Lieutenant Commander Bruce Bird, former Australian Naval Defence Attaché to Singapore, who laid the wreath to Major William Alston Tebbutt at Muntok in 2018 in thanks for Tebbutt's vital role in helping to locate survivors at Belalau Camp in September 1945.

Thoughts of our loved ones are our guiding stars.

Internee Gordon Reis

THE EVACUATION OF SINGAPORE TO THE PRISON CAMPS OF SUMATRA
EYEWITNESS ACCOUNTS OF TRAGEDY AND SUFFERING DURING WW2

JUDY BALCOMBE

Pen & Sword
MILITARY

AN IMPRINT OF PEN & SWORD BOOKS LTD.
YORKSHIRE - PHILADELPHIA

First published in Great Britain in 2023 by
PEN AND SWORD MILITARY
An imprint of
Pen & Sword Books Ltd
Yorkshire - Philadelphia

Copyright © Judy Balcombe, 2023

ISBN 978 1 39906 715 7

The right of Judy Balcombe to be identified as the Author of this work has been asserted by her in accordance with the Copyright, Designs and Patents Act 1988.

A CIP catalogue record for this book is available from the British Library.

All rights reserved. No part of this book may be reproduced or transmitted in any form or by any means, electronic or mechanical including photocopying, recording or by any information storage and retrieval system, without permission from the Publisher in writing.

Typeset in Times New Roman 10/12 by
SJmagic DESIGN SERVICES, India.
Printed and bound in the UK by CPI Group (UK) Ltd.

Pen & Sword Books Ltd incorporates the Imprints of Pen & Sword Archaeology, Atlas, Aviation, Battleground, Discovery, Family History, History, Maritime, Military, Naval, Politics, Railways, Select, Transport, True Crime, Fiction, Frontline Books, Leo Cooper, Praetorian Press, Seaforth Publishing, Wharncliffe and White Owl.

For a complete list of Pen & Sword titles please contact

PEN & SWORD BOOKS LIMITED
George House, Units 12 & 13, Beevor Street, Off Pontefract Road,
Barnsley, South Yorkshire, S71 1HN, England
E-mail: enquiries@pen-and-sword.co.uk
Website: www.pen-and-sword.co.uk

or

PEN AND SWORD BOOKS
1950 Lawrence Rd, Havertown, PA 19083, USA
E-mail: uspen-and-sword@casematepublishers.com
Website: www.penandswordbooks.com

Contents

Foreword, Mrs Rosemary Fell	vii
Preface – Thoughts From my Garden	ix
Ocean Waves	1
Love Comes Before a Fall	3
Escape to the East	7
The Garden of Eden	12
Days of Gold	15
Too Late	22
Some Letters from London	26
Destination Unknown	31
A Catastrophe Beyond Measure	33
Bangka Island	42
Palembang	51
On Severed Wings	69
Where is My Cat?	72
Over	82
The Whole Horrible Episode	85
The Chain of Destiny	90
The Lost Graves of Muntok	92
Where are They Now?	100
Our Journey	103

THE EVACUATION OF SINGAPORE

The End of the Road	109
Remember Me	118
Examining the Past	140
Chichester, October 2013	142
Positive Action	146
The Kindness of Strangers	149
Belalau	151
Remember Always	154
Muntok Peace Museum, September 2015	156
75th Anniversary Gathering, Radji Beach, Muntok	160
Walk for Humanity, Radji Beach, February 2018	163
The Origin and Location of Radji Beach	166
An End to War and a True Peace	171
Pimikir, Reflections	173
Poems	176
Selamat Tinggal – Goodbye and Peace Be With You	178
Terima Kasih (Thank You)	179
Acknowledgements	180
Bibliography	181

Foreword

As a founder and secretary of the Malayan Volunteers Group, I am pleased to introduce this book, which tells a tragic story but gives hope for the future. The Malayan Volunteers Group (MVG) developed from an informal gathering of a few British Malayan friends who had lived and worked in pre-war Malaya and were veterans of the Malayan Volunteer Civil Defence Forces. This was the start of the MVG, which now has a worldwide membership in the United Kingdom, Australia, New Zealand, Canada, the United States of America, Malaysia and Singapore. Our quarterly newsletter *Apa Khabar* (What's News) prints current events, anniversary services and ceremonies, wartime diaries and other relevant records and stories.

The MVG commemorates both military Far East Prisoners of War (FEPoW) and the civilian internees, whose history is less well known. The civilian men, women and children who had not escaped from Singapore before capitulation on 15 February 1942 were held in Changi Prison and later in Sime Road Camp. They suffered many of the hardships faced by the military PoWs... gross overcrowding, inadequate food, medicines and medical care and harsh treatment by the Japanese guards. Like the FEPoWs, many civilians died.

However, the fate of the many thousands who were evacuated from Singapore – especially in the last few days before Singapore fell – was far worse. Over one hundred small boats were bombed and sunk by the Japanese, with a loss of between 4,000 and 5,000 lives. Of those who struggled ashore on Bangka Island, some, including twenty-one Australian Army nurses, were massacred on the beach. Others were captured by the Japanese and interned in squalid conditions in Muntok and later in Palembang and Belalau on the mainland of Sumatra.

The many internees who died in Muntok were buried or reburied in graves in the town cemetery. The graves were initially well maintained but after the war fell into disrepair, and the land was covered by houses and a petrol station. In 1981, the remains of the women internees were re-interred in a communal grave in the Catholic cemetery. Thanks to the tireless efforts of MVG members Margie Caldicott and Judy Balcombe, the names of the civilians who died in Muntok camps and who remain there are now inscribed on plaques on this communal grave.

Today, Muntok has taken its wartime history to heart through the kindness of the people of Muntok and historians from the Timah Tinwinning Museum. The 'Walk for Humanity' each 16 February in memory of all who suffered in this area

THE EVACUATION OF SINGAPORE

is a unique experience of all nationalities and religions coming together in the spirit of reconciliation and peace and is a lesson to the world.

The Malayan Volunteers Group is pleased and humbled to be part of this moving annual event and to support prisoners' families in their understanding of the past.

I would like to end with the following sentiments expressed in this very old Chinese proverb, which encapsulates the hopes and aspirations for peace in the world:

> If there be righteousness in the heart, there will be beauty in the character.
>
> If there is beauty in the character, there will be harmony in the home.
>
> If there is harmony in the home, there will be order in the nation.
>
> When there is order in each nation, there will be peace in the world.

Mrs Rosemary Fell, BEM
Malayan Volunteers Group

Preface

Thoughts From my Garden

This story began as a personal journey. My father never spoke of his childhood in Malaya or of losing his father in a Sumatran prison camp in the Second World War. I sought and uncovered first my great-grandfather, learning how his infidelities once brought him to work for a sultan. I found his son, my grandfather, in this tropical paradise and followed him to a place of unbelievable horror, where I located his grave. Unexpectedly, I found others on a similar quest. These pages tell our story and of how many people have become a group of friends trying to build something positive from the tragedy of the Second World War.

I will describe how the war affected many families, take you to the wartime locations and reveal this important but previously little-described history. I hope you will be inspired to know how prisoners' families are trying to heal the anguish of the past and to help others today.

In February 1942, up to 5,000 men, women and children died at sea when more than one hundred boats carrying evacuees from Singapore were sunk by Japanese planes and warships off the coast of Sumatra. The evacuation is sometimes known as 'Singapore's Dunkirk', but, unlike Dunkirk, this was a most dreadful disaster.

Following the bombing of their vessel, twenty-one Australian Army nurses, civilians and around sixty Allied servicemen who reached the shore were massacred on Radji Beach near Muntok on Bangka Island, Indonesia, on 16 February 1942. One thousand shipwreck survivors were placed into harsh prison camps, where they were joined by Dutch families who had been working in Indonesia. In the following three-and-a-half-years, many died from malaria, dysentery, beriberi and starvation. My grandfather was one of those victims who died in camp. For survivors and for families, life was altered forever.

Today we are engaged in a different war, against Covid 19. We have been faced with fear and the reality of this killer virus. Our movements were restricted, many have died and we did not know what the next day would bring. And yet, the human spirit is resilient and resourceful. Confined to home, people met online. They began to garden, to cook and to take up new hobbies. I decided it was necessary to tell this story while I was able.

Similarly, in the harsh, unhealthy and isolated Japanese prison camps of Muntok, Palembang and Belalau, people kept busy and active. They cheered their friends and cared for the sick. They read and wrote newsletters and poems. They kept secret diaries and learned languages. They drew, plucked threads from tattered

THE EVACUATION OF SINGAPORE

clothes and embroidered with one shared needle. They prayed. They made gifts for one another, learned to read music and to sing. They picked wildflowers and watched sunrises and sunsets. In the midst of sickness, suffering and death, they persevered and never gave up hope that this would end.

A short time ago, before Covid, we visited Muntok for the annual Walk for Humanity, now held near the site of the 1942 Radji Beach massacre. In this town and in adjoining Sumatra, hundreds of civilian men, women and children – our families – lost their lives between 1942 and 1945. Now at this ceremony, all present hold hands and walk towards the water, hoping and praying for world peace.

In 2020, Australian, British, New Zealand and Japanese embassies joined together to plant a tree for peace in the former Japanese camp commandant's garden. We saw some healing of the past and hope for the future.

At the Muntok Peace Museum, which tells the story of the war years, primary school children wearing headdresses of golden crowns danced joyfully for us. Muntok had become a place of education, beauty and happiness.

Now a different type of crown, Covid, a coronavirus is facing our Indonesian friends, ourselves and the people of the world.

Confined to my home in Melbourne during the Covid-19 lockdown, I walk in my garden. It resembles a jungle, a respite from worry, for which I am glad. There are palms, ginger lilies, a spreading loquat and great bay tree. My garden is peaceful. Bees explore the nasturtiums and my blackbird hops. There are vegetables planted in hope for tomorrow.

There is no time in a jungle. There is day and night, but things are as they were and will always be. In my mind's eye, I can see my shy grandfather planting rubber saplings in Malaya before the war. He talks kindly to the workers while my grandmother embroiders on the verandah. I almost hear the hum of insects and screech of monkeys and see my young father and his brother dancing naked in the rain.

I think of other friends' families before life wounded them so badly. Here are young Anthony Pratt's parents picnicking in a glade. I see Margie Caldicott's grandparents singing in St Andrew's Cathedral and in Gilbert and Sullivan concerts. Gordon Reis, who later wrote of his 'slow death from starvation' in Muntok Jail, writes his peacetime diary.

Neal Hobbs takes the wrong dark road to the hospital and delivers his baby daughter on the back seat of the car. An elephant walks slowly across the macadam surface, unconcerned. The original people, the Orang Asli, sell durians to travellers from bamboo shelters. Dappled paths lead always onwards.

We have the past to hold onto, and there will be a future. But how to best live in this present difficult time? As Auschwitz survivor and Psychiatrist Viktor Frankl taught, man must have a meaning, whatever trials he faces.

For the dying internee Dr Albert McKern in Belalau Prison Camp in 1945, his meaning was willing his fortune for future obstetric research. For Captain Sir Tom Moore, aged 99, it was walking in his garden to raise funds for Britain's National Health Service. We cannot all raise £28 million like the gallant Captain Moore, or

THOUGHTS FROM MY GARDEN

give away $12 million like Dr Albert McKern, but we can all look for ways to make the path easier for others.

As ordinary individuals, we have helped to deepen the well at the site of Muntok's former women's prison camp, to build a new well and carry out repairs at the primary school. We have built the Muntok Peace Museum, which has a website, http://muntokpeacemuseum.org, for those not able to make the physical journey, and in 2021, we donated a Covid ambulance to the Muntok Red Cross. And most importantly, we have friends and a new extended family in Muntok and around the world.

Many good people suffered in the Second World War, as in all wars. The full history of our families is now known, locations identified and lost graves found. The circumstances of this story, with its many unexpected journeys, were tragic, but I hope the later developments will continue in a never-ending spiral, bringing people together in the spirit of friendship and understanding.

We cannot change the past, but a group of people have become firm friends, working together to help a township, particularly in this time of Covid, and to create a place of peace.

August 2022

Ocean Waves

Ocean waves carried us,
away from battle and the flames of war.
Many were carried again into danger,
into the path of bombs and pain
and now lie beneath the ocean waves.
Ocean waves lapped the island prison,
soothing the years of hunger and sorrow.
Ocean waves bathe the shore forever,
anointing the memory
of those who did not survive.
Finally, ocean waves
carried the living prisoners home.

Ombak Samudra
Ombak samudra mengantar kami melepasi pertempuran dan bahana peperangan.
    Namun ramai pula yang hanyut kembali kebencana bahaya, ke laluan bom serta jalan sengsara di mana mereka kini bersemadi dalam dekapan ombak samudra.
    Ombak samudra yang membadai pesisir pantai di pulau sang penjara, badai yang juga menenangkan sengsara kelaparan dan kedukaan, tahun demi tahun lamanya.
    Ombak samudra yang kini senantiasa pula menguduskan pasir pantai ini, dan merahmati memori mereka yang terkorban nyawa.
    Dan ombak samudra yang mengantar pulang tawanan yang sempat berupaya bertahan hidup akhirnya kembali ke tanahair mereka.

By Judy Balcombe, translated by Raimy Che Ross

THE EVACUATION OF SINGAPORE

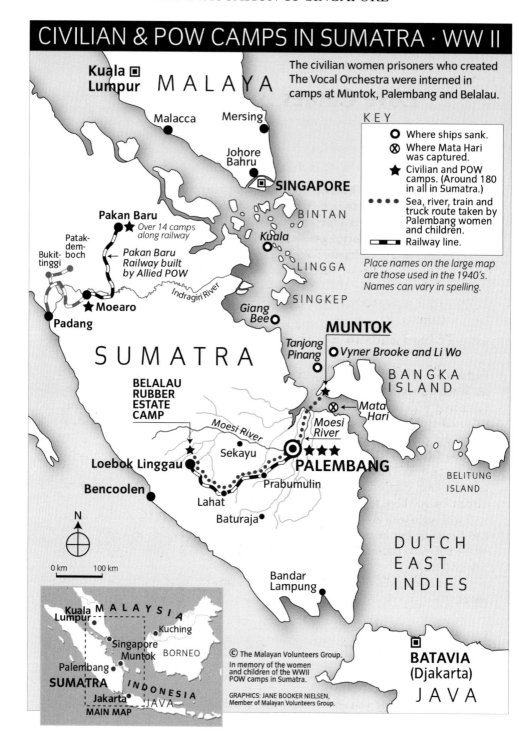

Love Comes Before a Fall

> Cross examined: I have been married four years, my wife is 27 years of age and I have two children; had no particular reason for giving the jewellery except I liked the look of the girl; I do not usually give young girls jewellery; I gave it to her because she was a pretty girl; My wife never knew of my intrigue with this girl until last night ...
> John Colin Campbell, Perth Supreme Court,
> Friday, 15 August 1884

One Thing Leads to Another

Perhaps life is a series of journeys, some we choose to take and others that befall us. When we begin, we do not know the final destination. The path may be smooth, or uneven with many obstacles. The roads taken by others can help or impede us. Looking back, we see the long way we have come. And forwards, we may eventually glimpse the future goal.

I would like to tell you a true story. It tells of journeys taken by many people over a long time. The way was hard, but the travellers had great courage and helped to carry their companions on the road. Remembering their suffering has given inspiration and hope to those who continue on the journey.

I will begin with my great-grandfather, John Colin Campbell. He was handsome and beguiling but intemperate. He ran from his responsibilities to another land, which indirectly caused his son to die. But it all started quite simply with a pleasure ride on a train.

These interwoven threads form the first of many journeys you will soon learn about.

The First Journey, Fremantle, Western Australia, 1882 – The Hat

I will start by telling you about a new hat, which a young girl lost in a railway carriage.

THE EVACUATION OF SINGAPORE

Perhaps you have been to Western Australia, with its bright sunshine and clear blue skies? Lilly, a young seamstress, had a ticket from Fremantle to Perth on the new railway. She bought a hat in the city to celebrate her trip – it was a big adventure for a poor girl. The hat was plain, maybe straw or felt. She planned to brighten it with flowers.

But returning home to Fremantle, Lilly found her hat was gone. She hurried back to the railway station and asked the stationmaster if anyone had found her parcel. There was no hat there, but Lilly's bright hair and flushed face caught the stationmaster's eye.

On another day, he approached her, saying there *was* a package for her in the ticket office. She unwrapped it to find not the hat but a brooch and earrings and a letter professing the stationmaster's affection. The two began taking walks together along the harbourfront at night. He told her about his life in England and in Africa, and she was enchanted. Sometime later, Lilly bore a child and then a second baby was expected.

Lilly was now unable to work and had no wages to give her angry father, a warder at the Fremantle Asylum. He took legal action against the stationmaster for seducing Lilly and decreasing his own household income. Confounding the matter was the fact that the stationmaster, my great-grandfather, already had a wife in Fremantle and two small children…

In August 1884, Lilly's father sued the stationmaster, John Colin Campbell, for £300 in Perth's Supreme Court. The courtroom was full, with standing room only. John Campbell denied he was the child's father and testified:

> I never seduced the girl in 1882, and it was not until the 15th of either April or March of last year (1883) that I became intimate with her; I can fix the date, as it was either the night, or the one following, on which the train was derailed at Guildford [.]

Letters from John Campbell to Lilly were submitted as evidence by the prosecution and raised much laughter in the court. Some lines from this incriminating correspondence read:

> Last night I tried to get in your place but I think I was watched all night. Once I walked along the fence when I saw a woman with a black shawl over her head and believe it must have been your mother …
>
> On Thursday night, I was turning down the passage on the way to you when I saw Miss Porter, who said she would tell my wife. I shall try to come tonight or surely tomorrow night … with unchanged love and devotion, I am still your JCC XXXXXX

And still more: 'I am very anxious to see you. In the meantime, accept my fondest and rarest love and believe me ever and always, your loving JCC', and signed with 26 kisses.

LOVE COMES BEFORE A FALL

The court case ran for three days. Another man was named as the child's father – this was disputed at length. Surprisingly, Lilly's advanced second pregnancy was never mentioned. In summing up, the Attorney General stated that:

> A tall, attractive, handsome-looking man like Campbell, one occupying a superior position in life to that of his victim, deliberately set to work to ruin this poor girl ... It was all very well for Campbell to have the impudence to enter the box and pretend to exhibit emotion at his wife's name. The miserable hypocrite put his fingers in his eyes in order to squeeze tears out of them, pretending to weep, with the intention of warping the jury's opinion.

John Colin Campbell, Fremantle stationmaster.

The judge added that:

> [A]s to the witnesses called for the defence, they were the most disreputable persons he had ever seen in a witness box; one of them even had the gross impertinence to wink at his Honour, while all of them frankly acknowledged they were leading lives of the utmost possible immorality [.]

Despite the damning letters and the strong criticism of the stationmaster and his acquaintances, the jury was not able to reach a verdict and the case was dismissed.

The Second Journey, to Singapore and Malaya

Although Campbell was not found guilty of fathering Lilly's first child, there was now a public stain on his character. He was made to resign from his position with the West Australian Railways on grounds of immoral behaviour. On 14 October 1884, he auctioned all his family's household possessions at his home in Fremantle – 'a most valuable collection' including quality furniture, rare paintings, a carriage and a pony, a canary and a cockatoo in their cages.

Campbell then left Australia, sailing to Singapore on the SS *Natal* on 23 October 1884 – the very day that Lilly's second child was born. The *Perth Daily News* reported that 'his many friends gathered on the jetty to give him three cheers as the steamer left the pier'. He took with him 'the highest recommendations from the Colony and it was felt his like would not be seen again in Australia'.

THE EVACUATION OF SINGAPORE

Did he ever return to visit Lilly? A family rumour holds that Campbell travelled by boat from Singapore to Scotland each year to see his illegitimate family, with children named after those of the Duke of Argyll. Perhaps the stationmaster had three families? Shipping lists show he made several trips alone back to Western Australia, where Lilly Kennedy had a third child in 1887. This baby son was left in the care of a 'baby farmer' while Lilly, disowned by her parents, worked as a servant. Tragically, the baby died from starvation aged 4 months, another case widely reported in the papers.

Before we leave Lilly, it is heartening to know that she later married a wealthy pearling captain, Frank Biddles, from Broome, who was the wealthiest man in Fremantle. Although she died young from cancer, Lilly lived the rest of her short life in luxury. Lilly and John Campbell's two daughters, Annie Flora and Margaret Charlotte, also prospered, marrying the Broome mayor and doctor.

Lilly told her new husband's family she was a widow and that her first husband, John Campbell, had been an Indian Army officer who had fallen downstairs and broken his neck. There was a grain of truth here, with Campbell having escaped to the East, and it was possible she wished his neck was broken! Lilly's real name was Elizabeth – Lilly was her pet name. John Campbell's wife was also Elizabeth, and by a twist of fate, both women are buried close to one another in Perth's Karrakatta Cemetery.

After Campbell sailed for Singapore, his wife Elizabeth and their two small daughters, Grace and Florence (known as Maie), travelled by boat to Geraldton, where her father Henry Gray was a wealthy storeowner. She may have planned to remain there but her father had been violent in her childhood, threatening family members with a gun and causing her terrified mother to jump from an upstairs window. Whatever Elizabeth's reasons, she, Grace and Maie later joined Campbell in the Far East.

Escape to the East

There is a thrill and something of awe in the thought that the very road one may be walking on or motoring through, was till a few short years ago, all virgin jungle, with giant trees and undergrowth so dense and thickly entwined that even the creatures of the forest found it difficult to penetrate. Huge elephants crashing through the thorny creepers, deer, tigers, wild pigs, the slow tapirs, bears, monkeys and panthers had all lived out their lives here untroubled by man for thousands of years.

In Malaya – the Singapore Free Press and
Mercantile Advertiser, 26 November 1929

For a moment I felt as though I had invaded some dreamland of my childhood.

In a little court at the end of our corridor, where a fountain splashed over a clump of lotus flowers and blue water lilies, a long-armed silver wah-wah monkey played with a black Malay cat and chased the clucking little gray lizards up the polished walls.

Tales of the Malayan Coast, From Penang
to the Philippines, Rounsevelle Wildman

Malaya 1884

John Campbell found a new job in Southern Malaya working as railway superintendent for the Sultan of Johore. He led a pleasant and interesting life in this tropical location. He lived with his family in Bandar Maharani, now known as Muar, in a large bungalow built for him by the Sultan. The Sultan dedicated the town, with its many lovely buildings, to his wife – Bandar Maharani meaning 'Empress Town'. The town lies at the estuary of the wide Muar River at the base of Mount Ophir. It is thought by some that this is the Mount Ophir mentioned in the Bible – a source of gold, diamonds and exotic animals.

The area was lush and prosperous, producing gambier, used in tanning and herbal medicine, and durians and other prized fruits for export along the river and

THE EVACUATION OF SINGAPORE

by sea. A local newspaper praised Muar highly, saying that 'all manner of goods could be bought there, from French perfume to German beer and boots which would do credit to Bond Street'.

The *Straits Times* reported in March 1894, after a visit by the Sultan to Muar that:

> Everything works well under the able and energetic management of Mr Campbell and the terminus is kept quite like a home-station. Mr Campbell shows great skill in gardening and the grounds surrounding the fine bungalow which the Government has built for him are a pleasure to look at by the passer-by.

The Sultan had built the Muar State Railway, a small wooden railway that initially ran for 22.5km, between Bandar Maharani and Sungai Pulai. The train comprised a steam engine, five passenger coaches and three goods vans. The fare was 5 sen per mile, and children attending the English school at Bandar Maharani were carried free of charge. There were five permanent and eight temporary stations along the line. In the *Straits Times* in January 1896, John Campbell advertised for 'a Bengalie or other Native fitter and erector, accustomed to locomotive work', for the Muar State Railway. He stipulated that testimonials should be provided and that 'none but competent and sober men of good character need apply'. Considering his earlier infidelity, he had definite double standards!

A Mr N.G.H. described the Muar State Railway in the *Eastern Daily Mail and Straits Morning Advertiser* on 3 January 1906:

> On both sides of the railway line there are betel nut, cocoanut and fruit plantations belonging to Chinese and Malays. The railway has a reputation of burning passengers' clothes by the sparks emitted from the funnel of the engine. Dato Sitiah, the State Commissioner, a person in authority, has also been a victim and lost a beautiful silk umbrella by fire caused by these sparks. The ticket collectors can always be seen with their uniforms burned. Could not some improvement be made?

In addition to his role as traffic manager and superintendent of locomotives, John Campbell was manager of the Muar Water Board. The local terrain consisted of dense jungle abounding with tigers, elephants, snakes and crocodiles. On occasions, tigers were seen to swim across the river and enter buildings with their open verandahs. The *Straits Times* weekly issue of 7 June 1889 reported that:

> A coolie carrying the breakfast of the overseer laying down pipes from the reservoir happened to see three tigers some distance in front of him. Thinking discretion to be the better part of valour, he made tracks home as fast as his legs could carry him, thinking it better that his master be left wanting his breakfast than that he should be the breakfast of the tigers.

ESCAPE TO THE EAST

Sultan Abu Bakar of Johore often visited Bandar Maharani from Singapore. He was fond of British traditions and conversed with John Campbell, who had been born in Scotland. By now, the stationmaster and his wife had five more white-haired children – the Sultan called them 'Campbell's children but my Angels'.

The Sultan may have heard Campbell's stories of his double life with Lilly Kennedy in Australia, and I sometimes wonder if these details influenced his own actions? Sultan Abu Bakar made many trips to England. As ruler of Johore, he moved in titled circles, impressing Britons with his generosity and his magnificent jewels. He met and became a good friend of Queen Victoria. In 1885, however, while in England, the Sultan took an astonishing course of action. He adopted the role of a commoner for a period, calling himself not Sultan Abu Bakar but 'Mr Albert Baker'.

MISS MIGHELL

As Baker, the Sultan began a relationship with an English girl, Miss Jenny Mighell of Brighton. She lived at 20 Devonshire Place, a lodging house, and it is possible that, as Baker, the Sultan took rooms there. Jenny only became aware of his true identity when a passer-by addressed Mr Baker as 'Your Highness'. The Sultan swore her to secrecy. They moved to Goring, where Jenny was known as Mrs Baker and believed the Sultan would marry her. Alas, this was not his intention and he returned to Johore.

In 1893, Miss Mighell tried to sue the Sultan of Johore for breach of promise of marriage. She claimed £10,000 compensation and the return of a diamond buckle.

The court details were widely reported in English and overseas newspapers, and I imagine that John Campbell read them avidly. She was unsuccessful on the grounds that Sultan Abu Bakar was deemed by British courts to be the Sovereign Ruler of an independent state, and as such could not be sued in another land. His status as a monarch was confirmed in the Western world by this leading case, while poor Miss Mighell faded into obscurity.

Sultan Abu Bakar later died at Bayley's Hotel in London in 1895 with Queen Victoria's physician in attendance. The Queen sent a telegram to express 'my deep regrets for one who has always been so kind to me and so friendly to England'. His body was embalmed in London and returned to Johore, where thousands attended the magnificent funeral procession, described as 'the most impressive ceremonial ever recorded in the annals of Malaya'.

Photographs show people crowding the road and extending as far as the eye can see. Among the crowd of mourners was the Sultan's friend, John Campbell.

Funeral procession of Sultan Abubakar, 1895.

THE EVACUATION OF SINGAPORE

Sultan Abu Bakar's son Ibrahim became Johore's next ruler. The young Sultan was regarded as clever and humorous. As a young man, Sultan Ibrahim had lost some teeth falling from a horse. The spaces had been filled with gold and diamonds; a dazzling display when he smiled. He had a number of European wives and fiancées – poor Miss Jenny Mighell had been born a little too soon.

John Colin Campbell continued in his role as superintendent of the Muar State Railways and Water Board. Newspaper reports record him attending banquets in Muar to celebrate Sultan Ibrahim's coronation and birthdays. Campbell took a keen interest in developments in railway engineering, particularly in a new style of locomotive produced in Japan. He wrote to the *Singapore Free Press and Mercantile Advertiser* in January 1902, praising Japan's mechanization and progress. He concluded this letter by saying: 'I merely mention these facts to shew that these [Japanese] people are determined to take a leading place in the world, both commercially and politically.'

We will learn later how prophetic and how sadly relevant to his own family experience these words were to be.

Left: Early railway line, Malaya.

Below: Jungle Matheran orchids, painted by J.C.C..

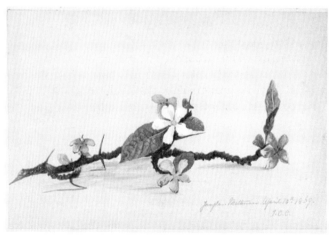

ESCAPE TO THE EAST

Singapore and Malaya, Early 1900s, Orchid Collecting on Mount Ophir

The tropical climate favoured the growth of both wild and cultivated plants. Flower shows were a popular pastime in Muar, and the Sultan of Johore was a frequent exhibitor and prize winner. Orchids were much-valued, exotic blooms grown in nurseries and native varieties found in the rainforest. John Campbell was a fine watercolour artist and produced many delicate orchid paintings.

Friends would venture on orchid-collecting expeditions, especially to the famed Mount Ophir, rich with rare vegetation and a great waterfall. H.N. Ridley climbed Mount Ophir to gather plants in 1892. He reported seeing many species of moss, climbers, orchids and rhododendrons. He also observed tiger tracks and deer footprints but noted that elephants had, by then, disappeared.

Legends surround Mt Ophir's cloudy peaks, particularly of a king in love with a fairy princess who set him impossible tasks. A traditional Malay poem tells us:

> However high is the trunk of the betel-nut tree,
>
> Higher is the smoke of fire.
>
> However high is Mount Ophir,
>
> Higher are the hopes of the heart.

In 1902, Campbell journeyed into the jungle of Mount Ophir to collect orchids, perhaps as a gift for his patron Sultan Ibrahim. He may have had 'high hopes in his heart' of returning with a rare Arundina Bambusifolia specimen valued for its large and brilliant blooms. Unfortunately, he caught a fever during the expedition, possibly dengue fever, which was first recorded in Singapore in 1902. He was taken by ship to Singapore's General Hospital for medical treatment but died there. Sultan Ibrahim sent a telegram to Mrs Campbell: 'Regrets, Johore'.

John Campbell's last journey was to the Bukit Timah ('Tin Hill') Cemetery in Singapore, where a white stone cross was erected on his grave. Forty years later, during the Second World War, this area was a fierce battleground between Allied troops and the Imperial Japanese Army. Campbell's grave and those of all others buried in the cemetery were destroyed. The cemetery records have been eaten by white ants. The stationmaster was gone from this Earth, but his actions in relocating to Malaya in 1884 affected his family forever.

The Garden of Eden

Some of our homes seem to have everything in them to make them perfect. They are filled with beauty. Music and art and refinement and the best things money can add are present; health and happiness and the gladness of social life …
Eastern Daily Mail and Straits Advertiser,
5 September 1907, p.3

I am fond of inventing happy endings to sad stories and like to imagine, too, sometimes, that I also may find my way back to my Eden one day.
The Singapore Free Press and Mercantile Advertiser,
17 June 1912, p.1

The Luck of Eden Hall

The Luck of Eden Hall is a fourteenth-century Islamic glass beaker decorated with swirls of blue, green, red, white and gold. Legend states that luck will hold as long as the glass is not broken. This Luck of Eden Hall is now in the Victoria and Albert Museum in London. Another Eden Hall brought Mrs Campbell and her family good luck for many years.

After her husband's death, his widow Elizabeth needed to provide for their seven children. As a girl, Elizabeth had experienced violence in her home. When she married Stationmaster John Campbell in Geraldton, Western Australia, her life had looked bright for the first time. The harbour was decked with bunting and fireworks set on the railway tracks in celebration.

Elizabeth could not anticipate her husband's infidelity with Lilly Kennedy some three years later. The resulting Supreme Court case was public and humiliating. Elizabeth would have had little confidence, no resources and nowhere to go except to follow Campbell to the Far East. Photos from her married life in Malaya show her looking sour and grim.

After the loss of her husband, Elizabeth gathered strength. She sailed from Muar to nearby Singapore and rented Eden Hall, a large home that she ran as a

THE GARDEN OF EDEN

boarding house for bachelors. The lovely house, in a quiet leafy area, belonged to a family friend, Ezekiel Manasseh, who also owned the Goodwood Park Hotel. Stories say he wanted to marry Elizabeth's daughter, Maie, although her mother would not permit this, and that the repeated 'M's on the staircase represent her initial. Instead, Mr Manasseh married Maie's sister-in-law Elsie (Trilby) Bath. The house is now the residence of the British High Commissioner to Singapore.

A Singapore newspaper article in 1907, titled 'The Garden of Eden, Music and Drama at Local Boarding House', reported a court case where Mrs Campbell sued a tenant who had left without notice due to excess noise at night. We read that Mrs Elizabeth Campbell, her seven children, staff, bachelors and a married couple lived in the house. The defaulting tenant complained of music and singing after 10pm, games being played in the hall and people shouting at the top of their voices. Mrs Campbell and her children were having a joyous time.

Elizabeth and John Campbell, Malaya.

Running the boarding house was a clever move, as her four daughters married some of the bachelors. Her three sons, however, needed to work for a living.

My grandfather, Colin Campbell, the oldest son, became a trainee rubber planter or 'creeper'. In this occupation, he trailed after experienced planters for several years to learn the craft of planting. He studied the science of the rubber trees, the language of the Tamil workers who tapped the tree trunks daily for sap and how to manufacture rubber sheets in the estate factory. Malaya was the world's major rubber producer, with the raw material sent around the world for use in tyres, road works, bridge building and many other purposes.

After some years, my grandfather became a rubber estate manager for the company Harrisons and Crosfield. He was then allowed to marry. Contracts did not permit planters to marry without completing several years of work and being promoted to a good position – even then, permission had to be sought.

In 1921, my grandfather came to Australia for a holiday. He took a room at the Federal Hotel and Coffee Palace, a large temperance hotel in Melbourne. He stayed for a month and met Anne McGrillen, who was working there as a waitress or maid. Anne was a country girl from a small arid farm in Rushworth, Victoria, where her father struggled to feed his large family. She was strong and bold and had come to the city to seek her prospects.

By all accounts, my grandfather was very shy. When asked what he wanted to order in a café, he would reply, 'Anything, just bring me anything.' Anne befriended him and conveniently lowered her age. I wonder if she talked to him about farming

THE EVACUATION OF SINGAPORE

Wedding photo of Colin Douglas Campbell and Ann Barbara McGrillen.

or if they just walked around the city? The end of his four-week holiday saw him become a married man.

Their wedding photo shows Colin seated nervously with clenched hands. His trouser legs are short – perhaps a borrowed suit? Anne stands tall and determined in a simple lace dress. She wears a large hat rather than a veil, useful for her future life in the tropics. However uncertain Colin may seem in the picture, life mostly treated them well for the next twenty years.

Colin and Anne sailed to Singapore to meet his mother at Eden Hall. Elizabeth recognised a fellow country girl and was quick to put the new bride in her place, saying, 'Remember, Anne, you are a Campbell now.' Such arrogance, despite her late Campbell husband being a wicked philanderer!

The couple travelled up to Malaya to Sarasawatty rubber estate, near Ipoh in Perak. The manager's house belonged to the estate. It was a typical spacious wooden bungalow, double storeyed and decorated with fretwork. Large, airy rooms were cooled by ceiling fans and cane easy chairs were set around to sit and sip refreshing drinks. Bright gold and crimson canna lilies stood ablaze by the front steps and along the shaded verandah.

Three children were born in the European hospital at Batu Gajah – my father, John, his older brother, Barney, and a baby girl, Marguerite, who died at birth. My father was tiny when born. He was wrapped in cotton wool soaked in oil, cradled in a man's shoe and fed drops of milk with a fountain pen. Somehow, with this care and the moist, tropical air, he survived. His father was Anglican and his mother Catholic, and so he was baptised into both of these religions. As a mark of respect to the workers on the rubber estate, he was also made a member of the Muslim faith. He always said he had three opportunities to enter Heaven.

Days of Gold

Take the coconut in both hands, raise it above your head and let the cool, sweet yet sub-acid water quench your thirst. There is no better drink in all Malaya. Some people drop whisky into the nut and drink the sophisticated compound. People who like that kind of thing, that is the kind of thing they like.

In the earliest of the morning, before the day awakes, monkeys chase along the topmost runways of the jungle, joying to be alive.
Illustrated Guide to the Federated Malay States, 1923.
Cuthbert Woodville Harrison

I think my Father had a largely happy childhood. He told of dancing naked in the steamy, tropical rain. He had his brother, his Mother and the amah who cared for him each day but most of all, there was his Father, whom he loved more than anyone in the world.

Colin and Anne Campbell with son John, Sarasawatty Estate, Perak *c.*1933.

THE EVACUATION OF SINGAPORE

My grandmother was an excellent cook but had servants to shop and prepare the family's meals, so this activity was precluded her. Tamil workers tended the garden, cutting the grass slowly with long scythes, and amahs bathed, dressed and fed the children – there was little for my grandmother to do. Her industrious nature turned instead to sewing fine mats and tablecloths for her home. She met neighbours for tea and cake and drove to the club for drinks at night. It was very different to her girlhood life in Australia, struggling against drought and hunger and cutting thistles on a farm.

She did not know, and no one knew, that an unexpected journey would soon begin, changing their lives forever.

But before this came, there was a long and lovely interlude, which we will call Permulaan – 'the beginning' – in Malaya on one of many such rubber plantations in the 1930s.

Selamat Pagi – Good Morning

The dawn is warm and gentle, the air like a moist bath and the sun shrouded in haze. The clipped lawn around the house is green, so green. Yellow and red canna lilies edge the path that flows to the gravel drive. The jungle lies at the edge of the lawn. Here, tall palms rise above tangled creepers. Insects hum in the still, peaceful morning.

Breakfast is laid on the verandah – tea, boiled eggs, papaya with lime juice and honey toast. The father rises early to supervise workers slicing rubber trees and catching the thick sap in small cups. He is a quiet, kind man with a ready smile. His early morning visits to the rubber tappers are always welcome.

The mother wears a light, flowered dressing gown and enjoys the cool of the morning. The children, washed and dressed, are brought downstairs by their amah. The children speak Tamil, Malay and Chinese, which they have learnt from the servants. They know some words of English to address their parents.

As they sit, a small brown sun bear ambles across the lawn. He visits each day in search of honey, standing patiently by the table. When the children have finished their meal, they are allowed to give the little bear a piece of sweet toast. He takes it in his small paws and eats it delicately. Then he turns and walks slowly back to the jungle, to return tomorrow morning.

After breakfast, the mother takes a bath and the father returns to work. The children visit the kitchen. A mother cat and her kittens drink their saucers of tinned Carnation milk. These cats have short stumpy tails, maybe descended from a Manx cat that came East with a sailor long ago. Mother cat hunts for mice while the kittens play with twists of paper on strings that the children tie to the knobs of the enamel stove. Cookie (the cook) in his white pyjamas, is fond of the children and does not scold them for interrupting his work.

Outside, the sun rises through the warm mist. The mother returns to write the menu for the day. Soup, chicken curry and rice, fruit salad. Most of the produce can be found in their garden, or Cookie may shop at the local market.

DAYS OF GOLD

Upstairs in the mother's bedroom, the ceiling fan turns slowly. The large windows, shuttered against mosquitoes at night, are open wide.

The children have a pet monkey, Bud, who comes and goes. He is small, with long legs and tail and an old man's face. This morning he enters the mother's room through the open window. He runs to her dressing table and is disturbed to see a monkey looking out at him from the mirror. He grimaces and so does the mirror monkey. Next, he bares his teeth. The reflection does the same.

Sarasawatty Estate, Bidor, Perak, Malaya.

Bud is angry and menaces his image with an ivory-backed brush. The other monkey also threatens. Our monkey hurls a pot of face powder, shattering the tri-fold mirror into a thousand pieces. Now there are so many angry monkeys looking out at him. He flings mother's long amber necklace, breaking the thread. The beads bounce and roll. He leaps to the bed, seizes the pillow and bites it. Feathers erupt into the air. Finally, Bud swings to the curtain rail, pulling it down in a tangle of cloth in one last angry gesture. He flies through the window to the nearby trees and swings away, screeching loudly.

After Bud's misbehaviour, the children play a counting game together:

> I went up 1 step – just like me, I went up 2 steps – just like me,
> I went up 3 steps – just like me ...
> I looked in the mirror – just like me,
> And there was a monkey – just like me!
> No, no, no! I am not a monkey!

Selamat Siang – Midday Greeting

Before lunch, the mother calls the syce, or driver, to bring the car. She must take her children to the dentist. They pass villages with small wooden houses, cross dense brown rivers and stop to let a buffalo pass. All the while, cicadas sing in the dense jungle.

Their destination is a town, with two-storeyed concrete shops. The covered walkways are cool and are raised to protect against flooding rain. They walk past rolls of bright cloth, pots, pans and baskets of fragrant spices.

Here is the dentist, his sign a large painted tooth to help those who cannot read. The younger child has a toothache. The dentist inspects and sees a hole. He places the child in the chair, tilting him backwards. He brings forth shiny tools and his drill, powered by his own feet like a bicycle. As he pedals, the drill spins.

The child wriggles and gasps but cannot speak, his mouth full of metal. The dentist is quick and the job soon done. Only then does the child cry. The mother takes the children to a sweet shop as a reward. She buys them shaved ice pyramids, with sweetened milk, jellies, beans and corn.

The English choir is rehearsing in the stone church. Their voices can be heard singing to the strong tones of the organ. The mother and children step inside the cool near-darkness. The sun's rays filter through the colored glass and dust motes dance. Pungent incense and flowers in tall vases scent the air.

The car takes them home past the racecourse. The sweating horses pound the dusty track. The spectators, men in white suits and topees and ladies in fine, light dresses, shout and strain to see the winner. If the horse is fast, it may be given a gold cup or be bought by the Sultan.

Near the railway line, the children ask to stop at a memorial to a brave elephant. They always like to see the sign that reads:

> THERE IS BURIED HERE A WILD ELEPHANT WHO, IN DEFENCE OF HIS HERD, CHARGED AND DERAILED A TRAIN ON THE 17th DAY OF SEPT. 1894.

The two boys thrill to hear the story of the brave elephant but grieve over his death.

Selamat Sore – Good Afternoon

The heat, the hum of the car and the drone of jungle insects send the children to sleep. This is the afternoon rest time. The mother and children lie on their beds under the ceiling fans and tented mosquito nets. The father comes from his work for a cool drink and reads his letters and the weekly paper. His long legs stretch out from the cane chair. His eyes close and he too is asleep.

Suddenly, a shout comes from the gardener – 'Tuan, Tuan, (Sir, Sir), come quickly!' The father follows the voice and runs across the lawn. A python has entered the chicken house and eaten the hens. It lies, engorged with plump round bodies, unable to leave through the mesh wire. The mother has heard the disturbance and joins them.

'Stay here while I fetch my gun,' cries the father. 'Make sure the snake does not leave.' The mother bravely places her foot on the snake to keep it still. The father shoots the snake and the diamond-patterned skin is later placed in a camphor chest, so the mother may have fine shoes and a bag made from it. It will be one of her few mementos of this life.

The daily rainstorm comes, sudden and heavy. The drops and wind slash the bending leaves. The children wake and pull off their clothes. They run outside and dance naked in the pelting rain, twirling and laughing with open mouths. The amah calls to them. They pretend not to hear her until the rain has stopped.

DAYS OF GOLD

Selamat Malam – Good Night

The parents dress in formal clothes – the mother in a long dress with pearls and the father in his suit. They kiss the children goodnight and drive through the night to the club, for drinks, dinner and dancing. The children eat their bread and milk and climb into bed. The amah, a young girl herself, lies on the mat outside their door.

The rain has stopped but the night is noisy. Small chi-chak lizards peep as they run up the wall. The wind scrapes the leaves outside and monkeys chatter.

Drums thud in the local village. A sudden harsh noise – could this be a tiger?

A child from the village and the children's dog have previously been eaten by a tiger. Large pad marks were seen on their verandah one morning. The children are afraid. Their amah is kind but small and does not carry a gun like their father.

They listen anxiously but finally fall asleep, dreaming of large animals in the darkness.

Above left: Off to the club.

Above right: Childhood in Malaya.

THE EVACUATION OF SINGAPORE

Sekolah – School

Boarding school boys, *c.*1933.

When they turn 8 years old, the children are sent to boarding school in Australia. Their mother takes them to Melbourne on a Blue Funnel Line ship. She has become elegant, wearing a fox fur stole with glass eyes and dangling jaws and feet; very different from the hard-working country girl of her youth. Now she has returned to Australia in style.

Her sons are given jackets and caps and left at school until their parents' next home leave. Here they learn to speak English well and not to cry. The older boy has been banished from his friend in Malaya, the Chinese opium-smoking gardener. The younger boy enters a ladies' toilet in Melbourne, thinking the sign 'Ladies' reads *Laki Laki*, the Malay for boys. They play sports and win prizes – they are given *The Meeting Pool*, *The Jungle Book* or *Just So Stories*, always books about the Far East, which is their home.

Their mother and father write often and the boys save the stamps. Their parents visit each three years and buy properties in Melbourne for their planned retirement in a few years' time. Their father comes to Australia in November 1941 for an operation and returns to Malaya to recover. He intends to retire after a further three years.

But the best-laid plans do not always come to pass. What did occur was unthinkable.

Harimau, the Tiger

> Tiger Terror in Perak
> A man-eating tiger is spreading terror in Upper Perak where already a Malay and a Chinese woodcutter have been killed and devoured.
> *Malaya Tribune,* 27 September 1933

> A report was made to the Ipoh Police on Sunday last that a tiger had been terrorising the inhabitants of a Malay village, Rambai Tujoh Saiong, and that it had killed one buffalo. It is still at large.
> *The Straits Times*, 31 July 1937

Tigers were much feared in Malaya – graceful but huge, powerful and stealthy hunters. Wild animals, livestock and humans were all prey for the hungry tiger. With its stripes camouflaged by the dappled light and vertical bamboo, the tiger would creep slowly, pause and strike, tearing flesh with its fierce teeth. As plantations encroached on the jungle, the tiger increasingly took man as its meal.

Pits were dug to trap tigers, with a live goat placed inside to attract the tiger by its bleating. Sticks and leaves were laid across to disguise the hole but the lid made weak so the heavy tiger would drop down inside. Then the tiger would be killed with knives or a gun.

Too Late

It appears that tigers have discovered the island of Singapore and some of them have decided to settle here.
Singapore Chronicle and Commercial Register,
22 December 1831, p.3

The tiger that has once tasted blood is never sated with the taste of it.
Spanish proverb

When the Tiger Salaams, the End of the World Arrives

December 1941 to September 1945

In 1941, a new tiger threat emerged in the Far East, as had never been seen before. The Imperial Japanese Army invaded Kota Bharu in the north of Malaya just after midnight on 8 December 1941. The Japanese leader was General Yamashita Tomoyuki, who became known as 'the Tiger of Malaya'.

This day began a co-ordinated assault on the world by the Japanese. As the hours passed, Pearl Harbor in Hawaii, Manila, Hong Kong, Singapore and Malaya were bombed, and the incongruously named 'Pacific War' began. It was to last for nearly four years. Hundreds of thousands died or were taken prisoner, and for survivors and their families, life was changed forever.

At first the British and Malayan governments told the residents of Singapore and Malaya that there was nothing to fear. They said the countries were well-guarded by the British and Australian armies and by the Malayan and Singapore Volunteer Forces. People were told that the Japanese were small, ill-equipped, wore thick glasses and were 'nearly blind'. It was believed that Japanese tanks could never manoeuvre along the narrow Malayan roads or paths through the rubber plantations.

But the Japanese, although bespectacled, were determined. Loyal to their Emperor God Hirohito and to General Yamashita, they were unstoppable. They rode down the Malay Peninsula on bicycles; their small tanks rolled on through rows upon rows of rubber trees. Battles were fought bravely but the Japanese could not be repelled.

TOO LATE

They hid in the dense jungle and fought their way down towards Singapore over seventy violent days. There was fierce fighting on land and bombs rained down from planes above. A Japanese aircraft flew over Singapore on 25 December 1941, dropping propaganda leaflets that read: 'Burn all the white devils in the sacred white flame of victory.'

Families in Malaya and Singapore were fearful. People knew of the atrocities committed by the Japanese in Nanking in 1937, when many thousands had been raped, tortured and massacred. News came that Hong Kong had surrendered to the Japanese on Christmas Day 1941 and civilians interned. The Malayan towns of Penang, Ipoh and Kuala Lumpur were taken.

Historians tell us that about 1,250 people died in the German bombing of Coventry in the United Kingdom, a fact that continues to shock us. Much less well known is that about 2,000 people were killed in Penang on 11 December, the first day of Japanese bombing. Half of the British air fleet had been decimated and Penang could not be defended. The town was captured on 19 December. Buildings were destroyed and burning. Bodies lay decomposing under ruins and could not be recovered for burial. Eyewitnesses described the stench of decay and death.

As the Japanese advanced, European women were urged to take their children and sail for Australia, Ceylon, England or South Africa. Ships carrying evacuees left in December and January – sadly, some were half empty. Many women believed Churchill's emphatic statement that Singapore could never fall to the enemy and so chose to remain with their husbands.

Men under 50 living in Singapore and Malaya were not permitted to leave the Peninsula without a permit. They were required to continue in their jobs, producing tin and rubber for the war in Europe against Hitler and to maintain infrastructure in the local government services and police force. It was compulsory for these men to join the non-commissioned ranks of the Malayan and Singapore Volunteer Forces. They underwent military training in uniform after their normal working hours, preparing to fight the Japanese with weapons and tanks. The commitment was serious – Gordon Burt, a member of the Singapore Volunteers, was awarded the Order of the British Empire on 1 January 1942 for his work with military armoured cars (tanks).

An Unexpected and Dangerous Journey

Here is a difficult question that I have not been able to answer – suppose you were going on a journey, a long and sudden trip away from home. Suppose there was a war. You have to flee and might never return. What would you take with you?

You are allowed to take just one suitcase, small enough for you to carry. You must be packed and ready to leave in one hour. What would you put in the case? The journey may take a week. A change of clothes, underwear, photos, a child's favourite toy. Other precious possessions must be left behind.

THE EVACUATION OF SINGAPORE

Suppose this journey does not take you to your planned destination. You do not know the war will reach you before your journey's end. Your ship and many others will be bombed and sunk. Carefully packed suitcases and many lives will be lost. Survivors who reach land will be imprisoned for years or will die.

I will tell you about this unforeseen voyage and its aftermath. All of the events are true and the people, real.

Above and opposite: At home, Sarasawatty Estate, Perak, Malaya, 1940.

TOO LATE

Some Letters from London

Below are extracts from letters written by Mrs Grace Goldie in England to her sister, Florence Maie Gordon, between December 1941 and the Fall of Singapore on 15 February 1942. Maie's husband, Richard (Dick) Gordon, worked at a tin mine in southern Thailand. Like many others, he and Maie fled their home for the perceived safety of Singapore as the Japanese advanced.

Grace Goldie and Maie Gordon were the daughters of the Stationmaster John Colin Campbell and the elder sisters of my grandfather, Colin Campbell.

These letters remain in our possession as they were 'Returned to Sender', opened and read by censors but never able to be delivered due to the cessation of mail services to the Far East. The first letter is postmarked 8 December 1941, the very day the Japanese invaded Kota Bharu in Northern Malaya. There is no mention of the evolving catastrophe, but there are some references that, in retrospect, were perhaps prophetic.

Gateway, Park Lane,
Ashtead, Surrey England

To Mrs R.H. Gordon
c/o Pong Mine, Takuapa, Thailand December 4 1941

Darling,

Elsie says you are spending your three months leave in Australia, leaving in July. You will get good weather there and plenty of good food. I seem to remember grapes at Christmas. I will stop writing in April as after that date no letters will reach you.

It seems as though we have been looking forward to seeing you for years and years and now it will be put off again till the end of the war. We shall continue looking forward to the meeting and nothing can stop us hoping. We shall all concentrate on thoughts of a good holiday for you.

Sallie and I walked to the village yesterday, such a misty, damp day. We met Mrs Hallett on the way there and Mrs Finch on the way back. Mrs Finch's brother who was thought missing is now a Prisoner of War. It makes us very sad as we know what German prison camps are like. I can't imagine a worse fate than to be a Prisoner of War.

Sallie and I went to Richmond on Tuesday. It is really good fun going by bus. We had a topping lunch, baked rabbit, potatoes and spiced pudding. Mr Carlton

SOME LETTERS FROM LONDON

was cutting a holly bush, the ladder slipped and he fell. It was six weeks ago and his elbow has not healed yet …

I must leave my chatter for today, dear. We shall be thinking of you at Christmas and New Year. God bless and keep you safe,

Grace E. Goldie

To Mrs R.H. Gordon
Eden Hall, Singapore December 15, 1941

Darling,

We were just completely shattered by the news of the Japanese attack on America and Singapore etc. Although it has always been in the back of our minds, we never discussed the possibility. And although we knew the news must be true, we still couldn't believe it at first. Naturally their having been in preparation for weeks, the attack was a brilliant success. But there's nothing to prevent us putting an equally brilliant finish to it.

One miracle has already happened – America is united and it sounds as though the Japs and Germans will have bitten off more than their stomachs can hold.

And we hope that you and Dick were able to leave the mine before all the trouble started and we pray that you will be safe no matter where you may be.

It doesn't bear thinking of if we let our thoughts run amok. As I have said so many times before, it is essential that we should be cheerful for the sake of all concerned. We think of John and wonder if he is in Johore or held up in Australia. And Claude. And what of Colin – did he get away in November as he planned?

This news is far worse than any bombing we have had to endure. We pray too that you may never suffer from air raids. It seems as if we must leave you all in God's hands and just quietly pray. I have just listened to the midday news and thank God things are not any worse.

How I wish I could telephone you. This may not be a Happy Christmas. I go to Mass but am still full of hate. Whenever I think of Hitler and the Japs, I haven't got a single Christian feeling. I could kill Japs and Germans with both hands.

Now to get back to everyday happenings – last week I had to miss writing to you. Sallie had her final extraction and came back complete with new teeth but a swollen face …

I must close, dear one, although I would prefer to go on writing as it makes me feel more in touch with you. Our fondest love and sympathy and may God keep you all safe. This goes for all relations and friends.

We are with you in spirit, Grace E Goldie

To Mrs R.H. Gordon
Eden Hall, Singapore December 19, 1941

Darling,

I have never known such a long ten days since the Japs started their offensive, or such a dearth of news. Last year at this time, we felt time dragged and shorter

THE EVACUATION OF SINGAPORE

nights would never come. Now we find suspense harder to bear. The other night, Jock and I were listening to the news and when I heard the Japs were only ten miles from Penang, I suddenly burst into tears. I horrified the family as I so rarely cry.

We think of you and Dick all the time and poor John who has been working so hard in his new job. I am heartbroken. It is a sad world today. Even if the Japs get away with it now, the day of reckoning is at hand and I feel all the comfort I can get from this.

I hope that Mrs Charles Hedsdon [?] and the children escape from Penang and that you are safe too. Shall continue writing in the hope that one day my letters will reach you.

We pray that you will both be kept safe from all harm. Our prayers and thoughts go out to all of you all day and throughout the night. And I hope all your things will be safe where they are.

Much love, dear ones, from us all and
God keep you safe, Grace E Goldie

To Mrs R.H. Gordon,
At Eden Hall, Singapore January 6, 1942

Darling,

I seem to have been going about in a dream for the past month. Before December 7, we were looking forward to a pleasant, quiet Christmas. Then when we realised what was happening in the East, all Christmas feeling seemed to go. I can't let you know how thankful I was to get your cable. I could hardly believe Sallie when she said, 'Dick and Maie are safe in Singapore'. You are now among relations and friends and whatever happens, you won't be alone.

It may be months before letters reach you. Yesterday I took down all the Christmas decorations and I don't know when I have felt so sad. No flowers this year, too expensive so we have bowls of holly instead ...

Many loving thanks for the cable and letter. They were much appreciated and helped us to carry on. I hope Colin, Claude and John are safe too although Colin will not be able to do much after his operation. I would much rather have air raids myself than any of you should suffer.

May 1942 be all you hope for, Much love,
Grace E. Goldie

To Mr R.H. Gordon
At Eden Hall, Singapore February 4, 1942

My Dear Dick,

Tons of loving thanks for sending the Straits Annual which has just reached us. This last copy will be so particularly treasured coming in the year of the Japanese aggression. The news of the attacks completely shattered us. Although we should have been prepared for them.

It was so kind of you and Maie to cable us. When the first cable reached us on December 20, it seemed a miracle that you had reached Singapore. We thought of

SOME LETTERS FROM LONDON

you particularly on Christmas Day and wondered how you were spending it. On New Year's Eve we toasted you in stout and lemonade.

Both of you are practical and capable. You can turn your hands to anything. We can't bear the thought of Singapore suffering air raids and you have all our sympathy. Sallie has the brilliant idea you could be evacuated to England. I wish, too, this could happen.

Imagine on Monday when we received another cable from you. This said 'All's well, chins up. God bless.' How thankful you are to know you are still safe and well and what a gallant fight all are making. We feel remarkably proud of you all.

We see by the paper that the Sultan of Johore is remaining with his people. Good for him. I hope they are all well-heeled.

I never received the letter you wrote when Maie was evacuated from the mine. I expect you realise this when you got no reply. Several of Maie's letters went down at the same time.

Once again, Dick, much love from us all and all good wishes. Looking forward to seeing you both one day,

God bless, Grace E. Goldie

To Mrs R.H. Gordon, At Eden Hall, Singapore, February 10 1942

My beloved Sister,

I came downstairs yesterday morning, prepared to write to you but when I turned on the news at 1 o'clock, I felt so upset that I could not write. I opened the front door, thinking it was Sallie but it was the laundry man. Instead of taking the laundry, I just felt compelled to weep. I had to tell him about you and Dick being in Singapore. He was full of sympathy and did his best.

It is no good thinking that a miracle will end this because it won't. Takes good, hard fighting.

I don't know if you or Dick were thinking of us particularly on Sunday? I felt someone was near and wished to know something. I suddenly felt the room full of spirits or thoughts. We may have to adjust ourselves – in spirit we are unconquerable and will remain so.

We received the parcels you sent us and have thought of nothing but your kindness. We will use the butter for special occasions but the sugar was lost, with the paper breaking. We will never forget your kindness and feel so badly now that we can't do anything for you. It wouldn't be so bad if we could be together. If we only had the seven league boots that you wished you had, or a flying carpet …

I don't suppose you will ever get the letters I have written but know we are with you always in thought,

Your loving sister,
Grace E. Goldie

Maie and Dick Gordon and her younger brother, also named John Campbell, were interned in Changi Civilian Prison Camp and Sime Road Camp for the duration of the war. An embroidered hibiscus sewn by Maie forms part of one of four Changi

THE EVACUATION OF SINGAPORE

quilts made by the women prisoners. This must have been created early in the war, as Maie developed a serious eye infection in Changi and lost her sight. A photo taken after her release shows her no longer elegant but gaunt like a scarecrow.

Maie's brother-in-law, Ezekiel Manasseh, the wealthy owner of Eden Hall and the Goodwood Park Hotel, died in Sime Road Prison Camp in Singapore, as did many older internees. Claude Campbell, John Colin Campbell's middle son, a merchant seaman, survived the war.

The Stationmaster John Colin Campbell's elder son, Colin Douglas Campbell, my grandfather, was the kind, quiet father; the rubber planter in this tale. His unexpected journey and the aftermath follows.

Above: Party before the storm.

Left: Car among the rubber trees.

Destination Unknown

Japanese progress down the Malay Peninsula was relentless. In January 1942, the mother packed quickly, preparing to leave her home and join her children in Australia. This is one of many sudden journeys families were forced to take.

The father drove his wife to Singapore, with others crammed into the large touring car. Each departing person was allowed only one small suitcase, so most possessions and treasures were left behind. The cars travelled in convoys, past streams of people on foot, through burnt ruins, noise and smoke.

Evacuees, Ipoh Railway Station, January 1942.

Several times Japanese planes were heard overhead, with bombs raining close by. Cars stopped suddenly and passengers sought safety lying in roadside drains. They could still be hit, but if people lay flat, limbs were more likely to be damaged than internal organs.

They finally reached the terrified crowds waiting to board vessels at Singapore Harbour. Wives and children left their husbands and fathers, parting in uncertainty and fear.

The children's mother boarded the SS *Narkunda* on 15 January 1942. Edging through the harbour, surrounded by smoke, falling bombs and dodging mines in the sea, the *Narkunda* managed to reach Australia safely. The mother was permanently deafened but alive and joined her sons in Melbourne. Those on other boats were not so fortunate; bombed and sunk, their passengers never reached home.

Intermission, Sarasawatty Estate

The father drove back to the rubber estate on the long, dangerous road. He and his staff rushed to burn the stored rubber and factory equipment, so these could not

THE EVACUATION OF SINGAPORE

be used by the advancing Japanese Army. He buried their silver teapot and tray in the garden, hoping to retrieve it after the war. The family's dog was taken to the veterinarian to be humanely shot, to protect it from torture.

One evening, the father wrote to his wife, hoping that she had reached Australia. He advised her of their finances and sent his deep love to her and to their greatest assets, their two young sons.

Sealing the letter, the father called for the estate postman. A slim Tamil man entered, and the father spoke to him gravely in his own language:

> Thank you for always doing your work well. You know there is a war and I must go away. Please take this money – I am sorry it is not more. Try to take care of yourself and your family. I hope I will be able to return here soon.

Many years later, I visited the rubber estate and met this postman, by then an old man. He told me the story of that evening, and I am happy to say his face and eyes smiled warmly with the memory of his former boss, Colin Douglas Campbell, the children's father and my grandfather.

The Question

Here is the question we considered earlier. Imagine that you are going on a holiday – what will you take with you?

Clothes, a toothbrush, toiletries, medicines, a hat, sunglasses, books, pyjamas, umbrella, passport, money, a camera, a pen and writing paper. The list is long but normally there is time to choose, pack and rearrange.

Now imagine you must leave suddenly, in a day or in an hour's time. Only one bag per person. You do not know where you are going or if you will return.

You think you are on a five-day journey to your home country. Sentimental items are important – letters, jewellery and photographs. Valued clothing, evening gowns, a fur coat. But this journey will not take you home.

You do not know this now, but you are about to see family and friends bombed and drowned. If you survive, for three and a half years you will wear one dress until it falls apart, sell your wedding ring to buy food for your children and wish to God you had filled your bag with malaria pills.

A Catastrophe Beyond Measure

In mid–February 1942, only a month after my grandfather had driven my grandmother to board the ship in Singapore, he made the flurried and hazardous car journey back through Malaya to Singapore Harbour.

In the seventy days since Japanese soldiers had landed in Northern Malaya, they had fought the British and Australian armies down the Peninsula and were approaching Singapore. There was violence, destruction and chaos. It was believed the Japanese would cut off Singapore's water supply and residents were urged to fill baths and receptacles with water.

Duncan Robertson, manager at Marconi radio depot in Singapore, reported after the war that: 'Until about February 9, male Europeans up to 66 years of age were not permitted to leave Singapore without permission from Mr Justice Aitken's Committee.'

The British government under Winston Churchill still believed that Singapore could not fall to the Japanese and could withstand a siege, but it was becoming evident the situation was critical. By 10 February, European civilians still in Singapore were suddenly told they were 'In the hands of God' and were urged to leave the country by whatever means possible.

Large and small vessels, steamers, gunboats from the Yangtze River, yachts and junks – all seaworthy boats – were commandeered for the evacuation and lay waiting in the congested harbour. The air over Singapore was thick with smoke from burning oil refineries and storehouses. Some had been bombed by the Japanese and others set alight by the British and Australian armies so contents could not be used by the enemy. In the dark night, the sky was bright as day, with burning flames 200 metres high. Loud bombing continued day and night – in the words of eyewitness Jock Brodie, 'the end of Singapore was in progress.'

Women, children and babies, families, older men, government personnel, planters, tin miners, sailors from the bombed British warships, *Repulse* and *Prince of Wales*, and soldiers en route to fight in Batavia clamoured on the crowded dock to embark. Bombs fell on the crowd and dead and wounded lay on the ground. Passengers were hurriedly transported out to the waiting boats in launches. There were tearful and frantic farewells as some husbands and fathers still chose to stay on shore.

My grandfather and many others pushed their cars off the edge of the wharf into the sea to prevent them being used by the Japanese. They also hoped the obstruction might stop enemy ships from berthing.

THE EVACUATION OF SINGAPORE

My grandfather left Singapore on the SS *Giang Bee* with nearly 300 others. The *Giang Bee* was a former cargo ship requisitioned into military service. There were no passenger cabins and little deck space. Passengers rushed to board from the launches, hauling their bags up swaying ladders. Suitcases fell open, strewing possessions on the ground – there was no time to retrieve them.

More than one hundred large and small boats carrying evacuees left Singapore between 12 and 15 February 1942, just before the island fell to the Japanese on the 15th. Of these vessels, all but twenty were bombed and sunk by Japanese planes and warships as they passed down the South China Sea and the Bangka Strait along the coast of Sumatra. Accurate records were not able to be kept in the chaos. It is not known exactly how many people were on board, but it is thought that between 4,000 and 5,000 passengers and crew lost their lives as these ships went down.

The British code books had been destroyed, and decoding apparatus had been dismantled and thrown into Singapore Harbour so the Japanese would not know that earlier messages had been intercepted. It was thus not possible for Singapore to receive urgent Dutch messages that Japanese squadrons were flying in their hundreds toward the oilfields of Palembang in Sumatra, above the paths of the evacuating boats. The fleet of enemy warships in the area was similarly unreported. The evacuees were entering Bomb Alley.

A bombed ship.

A CATASTROPHE BEYOND MEASURE

Fate of Known Boats Carrying Men, Women and Children that Left Singapore in Mid-February 1942

With thanks to MVG ships list researcher Michael Pether and the writing of Denis Russell Roberts, Spotlight on Singapore, husband of Ruth Russell Roberts, who died in Muntok Camp.

13 February
Siang Wo, bombed and beached, survivors 210, missing 1
Scorpion, gunfire and sunk, survivors 36, missing 115
Giang Bee, gunfire and sunk, survivors 70, missing 223
Redang, gunfire and sunk, survivors 31, missing 58

14 February
Vyner Brooke, bombed and sunk, survivors 106, missing 135
Li Wo, gunfire and sunk, survivors 8, missing 92
Shu Kwang, bombed and sunk, survivors unknown, missing many
St Breock, bombed and sunk, survivors 24, missing 1
Dragonfly, bombed and sunk, survivors 135, missing 70
Grasshopper, bombed and sunk, survivors 100, missing 165
Kuala, bombed and sunk, survivors unknown, missing, many
Tien Kwang, bombed and sunk, survivors unknown, missing unknown
Kung Wo, bombed and sunk, survivors unknown, missing unknown

15 February
Mata Hari, captured, survivors 483, missing nil
Fuh Wo, beached and blown up, survivors 46, missing nil
311, gunfire and sunk, survivors 14, missing 58
433, gunfire and sunk, survivors 6, missing 71
Pahlawan, captured, survivors 24, missing 2
Blumut, captured, survivors 29, missing nil
Yingping, gunfire and sunk, survivors 15, missing 57
310, gunfire and sunk, survivors unknown, missing unknown
Trang, scuttled, survivors unknown, missing unknown

16 February
Pulo Soegi, gunfire and sunk, survivors 25, missing 55
1062, gunfire and sunk, survivors 10, missing 38
Rentau, captured, survivors, missing nil
Elizabeth, gunfire and sunk, survivors 2, missing 24
Fanling, gunfire and sunk, survivors 3, missing 44
36, captured, survivors 22, missing 1
Mary Rose, captured, survivors 13, missing nil

THE EVACUATION OF SINGAPORE

17 February
Rose Mary, captured, survivors 58, missing nil
Excise, captured, survivors 7, missing nil
Hong Fatt, captured, survivors 52, missing nil
Tapah, captured, survivors 44, missing nil
432, captured, survivors 75, missing, nil
Dymas, captured, survivors 21, missing nil
Tanjong Pinang, gunfire and sunk, survivors 3, missing 164

And also the following (details unknown), together with many unknown vessels:

Jarak, damaged and scuttled
Chanteh, no further information
Malacca, presumed to have reached Rengat, no further information
Cecilia/Corelia, last seen making for Sumatra
Florence Nightingale, lost propeller and ?
Kulit, carrying civilian men and women, no further information
Andrew, seen heading for Rengat
Pengail, no further information
Tingarro, Sultan of Johore's yacht, reached Rengat, no further information
Hung Jao, no further information

The *Giang Bee* left Singapore in a convoy with two other boats, the *Vyner Brooke* and the *Mata Hari*. Local crew had been dismissed or had fled to their homes, so passengers worked shifts in the engine room. The ship's log indicates that my grandfather, although aged 51 and with recent abdominal surgery, volunteered to stoke the *Giang Bee*'s furnace. Amid the flames, the heat and noise, the sweat-drenched men shovelled coal faster than humanly possible, striving for their one chance of escape.

The Russian artist Vladimir Tretchikoff, later known for his famous paintings of the green-faced Chinese woman, had worked as a journalist in Singapore and was on board the *Giang Bee*. In his autobiography, *Pigeon's Luck*, Tretchikoff describes entering the engine room as a 'descent into hell'.

The boats left Singapore harbour, manoeuvring through the many sunken mines. They surged on, trying to travel in the cover of night and camouflage under overhanging trees on small islands during the day. Despite these efforts, the telltale hum of small planes was heard and wings bearing the red circle of the enemy Japanese were seen overhead. Bombs fell, killing several people and damaging the engine room of the *Giang Bee*.

At night, Japanese warships approached. Captain Lancaster ordered a white flag to be raised and all women and children to stand on deck, so the Japanese could see that civilians were on board. The attempt at surrender failed when a Dutch plane fired on the Japanese ships. Spotlights from the warships illuminated the *Giang Bee*, and Japanese loudhailers ordered the ship to be abandoned.

A CATASTROPHE BEYOND MEASURE

Women and children entered the lifeboats, but two of the four boats had been riddled with bullets, their suspending ropes shattered. This damage was not seen in the dark. These lifeboats collapsed into the sea, killing many of the women and children on board.

The warships next signalled their intention to sink the *Giang Bee* and fired shells into her stern. The many helpless passengers still on deck perished as the boat burnt and sank while others jumped into the water to their deaths. Captain Lancaster was among the many killed.

The Japanese warships then turned and departed, leaving hundreds in the dark water, dead and drowning. Internee Gordon Reis, who later died in Muntok Men's Camp, wrote in his diary: 'When I got into our lifeboat, the screams for help from around were appalling – mostly women's and children's voices now struggling in the sea [.]'

Only seventy people from the *Giang Bee* managed to reach Bangka Island. The other 223 people were missing, presumed dead. For two long days and nights, survivors struggled in the water against the strong tides, aiming for Muntok's two winking lighthouses and a fire lit by Australian Army nurses who had reached the shore from the bombed SS *Vyner Brooke*.

Passengers in one of the two lifeboats reached Djebus (Jebus) on the west of Bangka Island. My grandfather was in this group. Here, these people were hidden and cared for by Chinese villagers for some days until the Japanese military came in trucks and took them to Muntok Jail.

The second lifeboat, bearing Gordon Reis and others, landed on the Sumatran coast. A number of these passengers were picked up by the minesweeper *Tapah* while others, including the artist Tretchikoff, wished to continue in the lifeboat to Java. Tretchikoff was imprisoned in Java but released, as Japan and Russia were not then at war. The *Tapah* was soon captured by the Japanese and all on board taken to Muntok.

The SS *Vyner Brooke*, also in the convoy, was carrying civilian passengers, military personnel en route to Java and sixty-five Australian Army Nurses. These nurses had been evacuated for their protection by Army orders as the Japanese advanced and the rape and murder of British hospital nurses in Hong Kong became known. The *Vyner Brooke* was also bombed and sunk by Japanese planes. It is thought that 135 of her passengers and crew, including twelve of the nurses, perished in the bombing or were swept out to sea.

In his book, *Singapore to Freedom*, Oswald W. Gilmour describes the bombing of the many ships, including the SS *Kuala* and SS *Tanjong Pinang* near Pompong Island. He writes:

> Between the islands on the phosphorescent sea floated boats and rafts laden with people, and here and there, upheld by his lifebelt, the lone swimmer was striving to make land. All around the rafts and swimmers were dismembered limbs, dead fish and wreckage drifting with the currents; below, in all probability, were sharks and

THE EVACUATION OF SINGAPORE

above, at intervals, the winged machines of death. Among those who had escaped death from bombs or the sea there was not one who did not suffer from mutilations, wounds, sickness, hunger, cold, dirt, fear or loss and none knew what the morrow would bring forth. It was a ghastly tragedy, a catastrophe beyond measure.

Parched, sunburnt and exhausted, some from the many bombed boats reached land after hours or days, either in lifeboats, on rafts, swimming or holding onto pieces of flotsam. Weakened, they tried to look for fresh water or split open coconuts to sip the cooling milk through swollen, blistered lips.

However, they had not reached safety. Some, including twenty-one Australian Army nurses, civilians and sixty Allied servicemen were massacred on reaching shore, and for the others, many years of unbelievable hardship in prison camps had just begun.

'Horror off Banka', drawn by Lieutenant William Bourke, NZ Navy.

Map of Malay peninsula, Singapore, Bangka Island and Sumatra.

A CATASTROPHE BEYOND MEASURE

February 1942 Australia

My father was 16 years old in 1942, living at home in Melbourne with his mother, who was distraught. She had just arrived in Australia after being evacuated from Malaya, had lost her hearing in the bombing of Singapore and did not know if her husband was alive. Her elder son was serving with the Air Force in Egypt. To add to my father's stress, his school Wesley College, where he had boarded for eight years, was commandeered by the American Army in February 1942. He and the other students were relocated to a different school, Scotch College in Hawthorn, where pupils from the two schools attended in shifts.

It was a lot for a young boy to deal with. What did he know or believe had happened to his beloved father? Very little information was available in Australia and much was delayed and inaccurate. As late as 25 September 1942, seven months after the fall of Singapore, the *Sydney Morning Herald* newspaper reported:

> **MISSING FROM MALAYA, Tragedy of the Evacuation BUREAU TRACING SURVIVORS**
> Bit by bit, the pattern of the British civilians' fate in Malaya and Borneo is taking shape. Men, women, and children who were thought to have been killed or drowned during the exodus have been found to be alive. Others who were believed to have survived are dead or missing. The Giang Bee was known to have been destroyed …
>
> When all the evidence has been pieced together, the world will be saddened by one of the most tragic stories of the war.

1943, the Postcard

Families of the evacuees lived in limbo, not knowing if their loved ones were alive or dead. Then, in October 1943, months after it was written, a postcard arrived from my grandfather. It had been sent from a Japanese prison camp in Palembang, Sumatra, Indonesia. It was the sole postcard received from my grandfather during his years of internment.

This card told his family that he was alive and had not died in the bombing in the Bangka Strait – or at least, that he had been alive in March 1943 when the postcard was written. My grandmother sent a telegram to Colin's sister, Grace Goldie, in England on 24 October, advising her of his internment. The card from the prison camp had taken seven months to reach Australia. Until then, his family had heard nothing in the twenty months since Singapore had fallen.

THE EVACUATION OF SINGAPORE

The postcard reads:

> Colin D Campbell, Civilian Internees' Camp, Palembang, Sumatra, 15th March 1943
>
> My Darling, How are you and the Lads? I do hope you are all alright. I am keeping fit now and am holding my weight at 11 st. 11 lbs. Am short of clothes and shoes size 7 1/2. A Red Cross parcel would be much appreciated.
>
> Remember me to all. I am looking forward to the day when we meet again. Would give anything to hear from you.
>
> Remember Always Yours, Colin

My grandfather wrote that he was fit but in need of clothes and shoes. I believe he was in the water before being dragged into a lifeboat. When struggling to leave the stricken *Giang Bee*, he would have cast his shoes off to help him keep afloat, an action many performed and then regretted. His suitcase was abandoned and the clothes he wore, if not blasted, burnt or drenched with oil, would be perishing after a year in the tropical sun.

After the war, Muntok internee Duncan Robertson wrote:

> The Japanese only permitted us to send 3 postcards in 3½ years and I have reason to believe that 2 of these never got beyond the Japanese guard room of the Camp. We received a few letters – the first I received from my wife was the tenth she had written.

But what had happened after the evacuation of Singapore, since the passengers had left on their unexpected journey, and during the days, weeks and months that followed? We know from diaries and reports of survivors exactly what took place after the *Giang Bee*, the *Vyner Brooke* and numerous other ships were bombed and sunk and a few vessels captured and brought to Muntok harbour…

Bangka Strait, February 1942

As the *Giang Bee* foundered, the cries of the men, women and children struggling in the water stayed forever in the minds of all who heard them. The passengers and crew still on the deck leapt into the dark waves or stood helplessly on board as the boat sank beneath them.

Two lifeboats had sunk; the remaining two, each built to hold thirty-two, were overladen and held minimal food or water stores. A lady washed the face cream out from her Ponds cosmetic jar and passed it around so a few sips of water night and morning could soothe parched lips and throats.

People in the water grasped at ropes on the edges of the lifeboats, pleading to be pulled aboard. Most were refused in case the overloaded boats, already down

A CATASTROPHE BEYOND MEASURE

to the water's edge, should capsize. After hours of holding on and overcome by exhaustion, many let go, to drift and drown.

Mr Murray James Vijfhuis Miller, who had been on board the *Giang Bee*, wrote in his memoirs of a man treading water next to him, holding onto a lifeboat carrying forty-seven people. This man had had a recent serious operation and together with Mr Miller, was pulled into the boat. I feel this may have been my grandfather, who had stomach ulcer surgery in Melbourne in November 1941 and had then returned to Malaya to recover. Perhaps this may be how he reached the shore, instead of drowning?

William McDougall was on board the *Poelau Bras* when it was bombed and sunk off Java. He was rescued by a lifeboat after floating for hours in the sea, in what he called his 'own private miracle'. An American journalist, he kept diaries in the Sumatran prison camps, later published as three books, *Six Bells off Java*, *By Eastern Windows* and *If I Get out Alive*. It is through his descriptive writing and the memoirs of other survivors that we know much of what occurred after the boats sank and in the harsh years that followed...

SS *Giang Bee*.

Bangka Island

The ground of Bangka Island is rich with tin. When thunder strikes, the ground speaks loudly, 'Bang, Bang, Bang!'

> Nurse Describes Horror Sinking:
> The horrors of the night followed the sinking, when for 18 hours she and 20 other people clung to a broken raft in an ocean of oil, with corpses buoyed up by lifebelts floating nearby.
> Only the difficult tides, which prevented them from landing, preserved them from the fate of their companions, who were massacred on the beaches by the Japanese.
> Sister Veronica Clancy, *Newcastle Sun*,
> Monday, 4 February 1946, p.6

Bangka Island, February 1942

The *Vyner Brooke* was bombed and sunk near Bangka Island. Passengers and crew entered the few undamaged lifeboats, jumped into the water or slid down rough ropes into the sea, stripping the skin completely from their hands. The Australian Army nurses spoke of 'being surrounded by jellyfish', not knowing the 'tentacles' were strands of their own skin. Some reached rafts or held onto wreckage while others swam in their lifejackets. The long hours became days and nights as they drifted past wreckage, the dying and the dead.

Through the tropical darkness, the shipwrecked victims could see the blinking lights from Bangka Island's Tanjong Kelian and Ular lighthouses near Muntok. The lights were sometimes near and sometimes further away, as the waves pulled them in and out from the shore. One group of Australian Army nurses and children, seated on a raft, were close to land but were pulled back by the strong tides and swept out to sea. These people were never seen again.

Families were separated in the chaos. The father of a small child drowned, and his mother succumbed to pneumonia after reaching shore. The boy was cared for by the Australian Army nurses and civilian women, who believed he was called Mischa. This was in fact his father's name, which he called out loud, perhaps remembering his mother's cry as she watched her husband in the sea.

BANGKA ISLAND

Children Molly and Robin Bull were separated from their mother and sister when the *Vyner Brooke* sank and were believed to have drowned. Australian Army Nurse Eileen (Mavis) Hannah was able to give a message to Mrs Bull weeks later that the two had been plucked from the sea by Australian servicemen in a small boat. They had reached Java, where they were interned. The children survived the war and were brought back to Singapore by Lady Mountbatten to be reunited with Mrs Bull and daughter Hazel, who survived the Sumatran camps, and their father, who had lived through Changi.

In total, at least 100 boats were bombed and sunk by the Japanese over three terrible days. In 1945, post-war investigators found numerous skeletons washed ashore from this graveyard in the sea. Many further deaths occurred on land.

Finally, some people reached land, injured, dehydrated, exhausted, covered in oil and burnt by the sun. They sat and lay in groups along the western sands of Bangka Island or walked to the town. Groups of Allied soldiers were murdered. One thousand men, women and children who landed near or walked to Muntok town were taken by Japanese soldiers into the cinema and customs house for processing. After two harrowing days, they were imprisoned in the town jail and adjoining coolie line buildings.

Radji Beach, 16 February 1942

At an area now known as Radji Beach, a little to the west of Muntok on Bangka Island, an appalling event took place, which shook prisoners who heard of it and all of Australia and the world when it was known after the war.

A group of twenty-two shipwrecked Australian Army nurses from the *Vyner Brooke* had managed to reach the shore some distance from Muntok and gathered

SS *Vyner Brooke*.

THE EVACUATION OF SINGAPORE

here with several civilians and about sixty servicemen. They found water in a small stream and lit a fire for warmth and as a beacon for those still in the water. The nurses tried to care for badly wounded patients, making stretchers from branches.

The group included severely injured who needed hospital care and the entire group had had no food for two days. They therefore decided to surrender to the Japanese and request medical help and supplies. The following day, on 16 February 1942, the *Vyner Brooke*'s First Mate Sedgeman walked along a track towards Muntok to surrender. At the suggestion of Matron Irene Drummond, a party of women and children walked ahead to the town, led by elderly Australian miner Mr Dominquez and two wounded soldiers. This action saved their lives from what was to follow, as this group reached Muntok, where they were imprisoned.

Sedgeman soon returned to the beach, accompanied by twelve armed Japanese soldiers carrying a machine gun. The soldiers gestured to half of the shipwrecked men to move around a cove. After some time, the soldiers returned, wiping their bayonets and calling for the second group of men to follow. It was evident the first men had been killed and that a further execution was to occur.

Ernest Lloyd, a stoker from the *Prince of Wales*, and American brewer Eric Germann were the only male survivors of this atrocity. As the men were marched into the sea to be shot, Ernest Lloyd dived below a wave. He was shot in the scalp but swam away. Eric Germann was bayonetted but lay pretending to be dead. Both Lloyd and Germann testified to authorities after the war. Private Cecil Gordon Kinsley, a British soldier, survived the massacre but later died in Muntok Jail.

Vivian Bullwinkel, the only nurse to survive the massacre, reported that the Japanese then ordered the twenty-two Australian Army nurses and an elderly civilian woman, Mrs Betteridge, who had refused to leave her injured husband, to walk together into the sea. Matron Irene Drummond called to her nurses as they held hands and walked into the water, 'Chin up, girls, I'm proud of you! I love you all!' The women were struck from behind with machine gun fire and fell face forward, one by one.

The Japanese soldiers then killed the injured stretcher patients with bayonets and rifle butts.

Vivian Bullwinkel was shot but survived – a bullet passed through her body above her hip but missed vital organs. She lay stunned in the shallow water, drifting in and out of consciousness. On waking, she pretended to be dead until the soldiers had left. Much later, finding the Japanese were gone, Vivian struggled up the sand to hide in dense jungle. Here she found the injured Private Kinsley with severe abdominal and shoulder wounds.

Vivian cared for Kinsley in the jungle for twelve days, bathing and dressing his injuries with leaves and begging rice from local village women. The village men feared Japanese soldiers and turned Vivian away. Realizing they could not continue, Vivian and Kinsley decided to walk towards Muntok town to surrender, after Kinsley asked to spend his last birthday, his 30th, as a free man. A Japanese officer stopped

BANGKA ISLAND

his car and drove them to Muntok, where they were placed in the coolie lines. After several days, Kinsley died from his wounds, with Vivian by his side. She corresponded with his wife in England after the war.

Vivian entered the Muntok coolie lines (the old public works depot) holding a water bottle over the bullet hole in her uniform. She told her fellow nurses what had taken place, but they swore to secrecy as it was feared the Japanese would kill them all if they knew what horrors Vivian had seen.

While in Muntok, Vivian informed Major William Alston Tebbutt, a senior Army officer, about the massacre so this could be officially documented if she should die. Major Tebbutt had been in charge of the nurses on the *Vyner Brooke* but became separated from them in the water. He was transferred to military prisons in Palembang and later Changi in Singapore but followed reported sightings of the nurses and their locations throughout the war. At the end of the war, the Japanese denied the existence of the last prison camp containing civilians and the twenty-four surviving Australian Army nurses. It was through Major Tebbutt's persistence that there must be nurses still alive that Belalau camp survivors were finally found and rescued in September 1945. On their release, they were described as resembling prisoners from Belsen.

Nurse Vivian Bullwinkel.

Vivian Bullwinkel testified at the Japanese War Crimes Tribunal in Tokyo in 1946, when newspapers reported the full, terrible story. The Japanese unit responsible for the killings was identified by Vivian by three distinctive round gold balls on their uniforms. It was established that these Japanese soldiers belonged to the same Orita Battalion responsible for the many massacres in Nanking in 1937 and in Hong Kong.

Of the sixty-five Australian Army nurses who boarded the *Vyner Brooke* in Singapore, twelve drowned or died from wounds in waters of the Bangka Strait and twenty-one died when machine-gunned in the water at Radji Beach. Thirty-two nurses were interned with the civilian women in Muntok and Palembang and in Belalau camp at Loeboek Linggau in Sumatra. The nurses suffered dreadfully in camp but cared for others despite their weakened state. Eight of the nurses perished from sickness and starvation, four in Muntok and four in Belalau camps.

Radji Beach is known to residents of Bangka Island as English Bay because of the European people who were killed there. In addition to numerous intact skeletons, pieces of human bone washed up on the shore for many years, and the people of Muntok would not eat fish from this area for a very long time. They believed that the location had become haunted.

THE EVACUATION OF SINGAPORE

Radji Beach, Muntok (Teluk Menggeris, also known as Teluk Inggris or English Bay) and the cove around which men were killed.

People living near Radji Beach were terrified of retribution from the Japanese and abandoned their village. A villager whose family had helped either shipwrecked servicemen or escapees from the Muntok Camp was given £50 by the Australian government after the war.

The Alhambra Cinema, 17 February 1942

Further tragedy occurred in Muntok on 17 February 1942, where the 1,000 shipwrecked evacuees waited in the Alhambra cinema and customs house. Adversity had befallen all of the captives but another event was especially horrific.

Mr Vivian Bowden had been Australia's official representative to Singapore – the role now known as ambassador. He had left Singapore on Sunday, 15 February on the launch *Mary Rose*, one of the very last boats to depart. On board were other diplomatic figures and military personnel who had been ordered to leave. The *Mary Rose* carried the vital decoding machine, which Captain Mulock was under instructions to throw into Singapore Harbour to prevent its use by the Japanese. Without the machine and code books, the British in Singapore could receive no messages being transmitted by the Dutch, warning of the many Japanese planes and warships heading towards Sumatra.

Encountering Japanese warships off Bangka island, the *Mary Rose* raised a pair of white underpants as a surrender flag. She was captured and escorted into Muntok Harbour, where passengers were taken to the crowded cinema building. Mr Bowden's staff, Mr Wootton and Mr Quinn, accompanied him and became official witnesses to the events that followed.

Inside the cinema, Japanese soldiers were examining possessions. Mr Bowden spoke out in support of Frank Brewer, a British soldier being hit by soldiers for having an oil can for a rifle in the kit bag he was carrying. His own bag had been lost at sea, and he had grasped another, not knowing what was inside. An altercation arose between Mr Bowden and an enemy soldier. A second soldier then tried to take Mr Bowden's gold watch and identity disc.

Mr Bowden had grown up in Japan, where his family had a silk business in Yokohama. He spoke Japanese fluently. He asked to speak to a senior officer to explain his diplomatic status, as ordered by the Australian Government in the event of capture, and to request humane treatment for the prisoners.

Enraged, the soldier pushed and hit Mr Bowden and broke Captain Mulock's nose with a rifle butt. Two soldiers then took Mr Bowden outside. Shots were heard. A witness looking through a window in an adjoining building told of Mr Bowden being forced to dig a shallow hole and to collect a small bunch of flowers before being shot and pushed into the grave.

After the war, Frank Brewer was interviewed. An audio transcript describing Mr Bowden's fate is held in London's Imperial War Museum and is online.

The *Mata Hari*

The third boat in the convoy leaving Singapore, the *Mata Hari,* was bombed from above. People were injured by shrapnel but the boat was able to proceed. Flashes were seen ahead in the dark night – passengers believed it was lightning, but these actually came from the bombing of the *Giang Bee*, the *Vyner Brooke* and the many other boats nearby.

Soon voices were heard from the water, calling for help. The captain stopped and ordered a lifeboat to be lowered. Sailors from the bombed *Scorpion* were rescued and confirmed the bombing took place.

The *Mata Hari*'s Captain Carston tried to enter the estuary of the Moesi River on Sumatra's east coast. He wished to aim for Palembang, so the passengers could try to reach Padang on the west coast by train. He could not find a pilot willing to escort the *Mata Hari* along the river and so instead sailed close to the Sumatran shore. He hoped the larger Japanese vessels would not enter the shallows and that, if the *Mata Hari* was sunk, passengers would have a greater chance of swimming to land.

THE EVACUATION OF SINGAPORE

Despite his efforts, the *Mata Hari*, carrying 483 people, was surrounded by Japanese warships. A smaller boat nearby, carrying evacuees from Singapore and bearing a white surrender flag, was bombed and sunk in full view of the *Mata Hari*'s passengers. The Japanese then ordered the *Mata Hari* into Muntok Harbour.

Before people disembarked onto the Muntok pier, Captain Carston opened the ship's food store and encouraged passengers to take tins of food. These, together with their suitcases of clothing, were later a boon for people from other ships, who, having been bombed and shipwrecked, had lost everything.

The Muntok Jail and Coolie Lines, February and March 1942

After two days, the 1,000 civilian men, women and children, servicemen and nurses were taken from the cinema and customs house. They were marched through the town and crowded into the high stone walls of Muntok Jail and adjoining coolie lines (the former public works depot or quarantine station).

In the rectangular jail, cells opened off the four sides with an open area in the middle. There was a single tap that produced drips of water, and people formed long queues to fill scavenged drinking vessels. One man had a small tobacco tin to drink from, another found half a coconut shell on a rubbish heap. The Japanese issued dirty white rice in buckets twice a day, which the prisoners divided evenly, providing each person with a small handful. A few strands of vegetables added flavour but little nutrition.

Also in the jail were 600 Chinese workers press-ganged from the streets of Hong Kong by the Japanese and shipped to Muntok to work in the tin mines. These

Muntok coolie lines, former public works depot.

Chinese labourers were ill with dysentery and typhoid and were very poorly treated by their captors. Several labourers died each day in the jail. Eric Germann saw two Chinese workers go mad and leap onto the roof. A Japanese guard aimed his rifle and shot one man dead – the other was ordered down.

At night, the prisoners lay shoulder to shoulder in cells on cold, sloping concrete slabs. The jail had recently been used as a pepper warehouse, and a few managed to find an old sack to lie on. The cells were very cramped – if one person turned over at night, everyone was disturbed.

The Australian and English army nurses, civilian nurses and doctors in the coolie lines tried to help the wounded. Many had been injured by bombs, gun fire and burning oil, others burnt and blistered by the sun. People who had stripped the skin from their hands as they slid down ropes into the water could not raise their arms to feed themselves and so were fed by friends. Captive doctors performed a double leg amputation under only morphine sedation. Their patient survived the surgery only to die from dysentery.

Everything was done to help injured Private Kinsley, who had entered the jail with Vivian Bullwinkel, but his shoulder wound was infected, and with no proper hospital care or medicine available, he could not be saved. He died two days after reaching Muntok.

Vivian Bullwinkel's injuries were kept secret from the Japanese and, incredibly, she survived. So too did Stoker Ernest Lloyd and Eric Germann, both shot and bayonetted on Radji Beach. Vivian's army nurse uniform, with bullet holes and stains of blood, is now on display in the Australian War Memorial in Canberra. In Muntok today, she is revered and known as 'The Vivian' and commemorated in the Vivian Bullwinkel Galleri in the Timah Museum.

The captive men in Muntok Jail were set to work by the Japanese. Some were made to unload Japanese ships at the Muntok pier while others were taken in trucks in the darkness to an airfield. Here, the men were stood facing deep trenches, believing they were about to be shot and buried.

Instead, the Japanese handed them shovels, ordering them to fill the pits, dug earlier by the Dutch to disrupt the aerodrome and prevent its use. The captive men were forced from their uncomfortable sleep each day at 4.30am and made to work until 11pm, labouring by the light of flares.

The Muntok airfield had been established in 1919 for the Australian flyer Sir Ross Smith, Lawrence of Arabia's pilot. It was used by many pioneer aviators, including Mrs Lores Bonney, who landed in Muntok in 1937 to escape a storm. Mrs Bonney received the Order of the British Empire as the first woman to fly around Australia and from Australia to England. Now this airfield was being repaired by slaves.

The Moesi River, Sumatra, April 1942

After some weeks in Muntok Jail, the men, women and children were transported in stinking coal barges across the Bangka Strait and up Sumatra's wide Moesi

THE EVACUATION OF SINGAPORE

River to the city of Palembang. Although not a great distance, the journey lasted more than twelve hours and was exhausting and uncomfortable.

The captives' only nourishment on the voyage was a rice ball and a cup of cold black tea. They shielded from the tropical sun in the dark, reeking hold.

Dysentery with cramps and frequent diarrhoea had begun to strike. The 'toilet' was a wooden board suspended high above the waves. The prisoners had to use these primitive facilities in full view of each other and the Japanese guards and risked falling overboard. The women's friends tried to shield them with clothing.

The prisoners did not know they would make this dreadful trip several more times during their years of imprisonment – each journey finding them increasingly more frail and ill and having lost many of their friends to sickness and starvation.

Palembang

The Moesi River snakes from the ocean of the Bangka Strait through rancid and desolate mangrove swamps to the oil-rich fields of Pladjoe and Sungei Geron.

We were given rice and, sometimes, a one-inch square piece of fish or meat.

Internee Harry Walker

Old Dutch house, area of Irenelaan, Palembang, former women's camp.

THE EVACUATION OF SINGAPORE

Palembang Jail, civilian men's camp from 1942 to 1943. British nurses and a Dutch doctor's wife were later held here for six months on no known charge.

Palembang, Sumatra 1942 to 1944

In Palembang, the captives were first taken to a disused school at Bukit Besar (Big Hill) near the centre of the city. The British and Australian male military prisoners of war had arrived before the nurses and civilian women and children and had prepared a hot meal for them – their first proper food in weeks (and indeed for some years afterwards). The civilians, nurses and soldiers were held together at Bukit Besar for several days and then separated.

The soldiers were then imprisoned in the former Mulo and Chung Wha schools near the Moesi River and were forced to work in Palembang city. Nurses and civilian women and children were first taken to a cluster of abandoned Dutch cottages surrounded by barbed wire and shortly after to another such enclosed compound. Towers manned by Japanese guards stood at each corner of the wire fence. The civilian men were confined in the Palembang town jail.

Palembang Jail and Pladjoe

Captured in Palembang after his launch was fired on and sunk in the Moesi River, engineer Gordon Burt was first interrogated by the Kempeitai, the Japanese military

PALEMBANG

police. He was held in solitary confinement and placed in a military prison camp before being imprisoned with Allied civilians.

He was horrified to find himself in Palembang Jail, dirty and overcrowded and with no facilities. He slept with three others in a crowded cell on concrete slabs with no bedding, next to a foul open latrine drain. Like internee William McDougall, Burt scrounged for possessions on the jail rubbish heap, finding a broken cup and water bottle to use as utensils.

Some 480 Dutch, British and Eurasian men were first imprisoned in the jail, built for 150 local prisoners. They included the men brought on barges from Muntok, the Muntok priest, the Bishop of Palembang with Catholic brothers, Dutch administrators, officials from Lahat and later, the workers from Pladjoe.

A group of about 160 soldiers and civilians was taken by the Japanese from Muntok to work on the oil fields at Pladjoe on the Moesi River. The refineries and airfields had been deliberately damaged by Dutch workers at the start of the war as part of a scorched earth policy and further destroyed in the Battle of Palembang. At Pladjoe, the captives were made to unload heavy pipes and boxes of cement from ships and to restore the oil refineries and airfields. The work was arduous and the days very long. Food and conditions were poor and dysentery (serious, infectious diarrhoea) soon killed several men. Their friends said simple prayers and burnt the bodies on the local golf course.

Prisoner Duncan Robertson wrote that after a month's labour, only twenty of the 160 men sent to Pladjoe remained fit for heavy work. After two months, the civilian men were brought from Pladjoe to join the other internees in Palembang Jail. Journalist McDougall wrote of the arrival of the ragged newcomers as they hobbled through the gates into the jail yard, limping, on crutches, held up by others or carried in on stretchers. The horrified watching prisoners were aware that, despite their previous efforts at hygiene, dysentery cases had now arrived at the jail.

Stilt houses, Moesi River, Palembang.

THE EVACUATION OF SINGAPORE

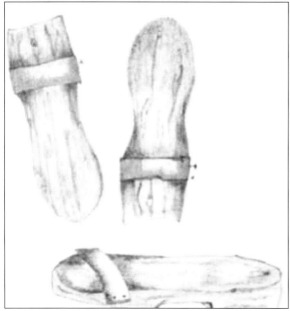

Above: Sultan Mahmud Badaruddin 11 Museum, Palembang, former Japanese headquarters.

Left: Handmade wooden sandals or 'trompers', for walking through mud (painted by Judy Fowler).

PALEMBANG

Irenelaan, the Old Dutch Houses Women's Prison Camp, Palembang 1 April 1942 to 20 September 1943

Approximately 500 civilian women and children, Australian and British army nurses and forty Dutch Catholic nuns were moved to the 18 abandoned Dutch houses, whose tenants had fled to Java. The houses were in two Palembang streets named Irenelaan and Bernhardlaan (Irene and Bernard Lanes) after the Dutch princess and prince. The women called this camp 'the Dutch Houses Camp' or 'Irenelaan'. Ironically, the name Irene means 'Peace'.

The small houses had been home to Dutch workers and their families and each had three rooms. But now, thirty to forty people were placed in each house and fifteen crowded into the adjoining carports. The women struggled to preserve some semblance of order in their lives. They made use of every article left behind by the former householders. A bowl, a cracked plate or a discarded stove thrown into the yard all became precious and valued items. A baby's cot served as a bed for one small nurse until it was more needed for firewood.

The women formed small cooking groups or kongsies. They worked hard chopping wood for fires and cooking the meagre rations of rice, rotting vegetables and occasional fragments of meat. The rice was husked and white with reduced nutrition. There was no bread and almost no fats.

Firewood and food were brought into camp in trucks by the Japanese. The slimy vegetables and a small slab of stinking meat to feed the whole camp were flung out onto the hot and dusty road, where a guard would hack a piece for each house with his penknife. There was no soap and no modern facilities, but somehow these women, who only weeks before had had their own homes and servants, managed to care for themselves and their children.

In addition to the British and Australian evacuees from Singapore, many Dutch women and children who had lived in Sumatra were interned in the Palembang camp. They had been seized from their homes by the Japanese and brought into the prison camps in trucks. Unlike the bombed and shipwrecked evacuees, the Dutch often had possessions – clothes, bedding, furniture, food and money. The other penniless captives were sometimes able to work for the Dutch, washing clothes, cooking, chopping wood, cutting hair or minding children for a few coins. They could then try to buy a little extra food from shopkeepers occasionally allowed into the camp or, at great risk to both seller and purchaser, from illegal traders who came up the barbed wire. Rings, jewellery, watches and personal effects were also traded for food.

The women were forced to bow to all Japanese nearby. They were made to line up for roll calls, known as *Tenko*, standing in the hot sun for many hours. *Tenko* roll calls could occur several times a day or in the middle of the night, for no reason. The women were slapped and beaten harshly for not bowing deeply enough or for any perceived transgression. Some women had their teeth knocked out or their jaws broken by Japanese guards.

THE EVACUATION OF SINGAPORE

The guards supervised all their activities within the camp. There was no privacy, not even for bathing or sleep – the guards watched as the women washed themselves and lifted their bedcovers to look at them during the night.

The internees and Army nurses shared the very little they had. The shipwrecked victims had no possessions and sometimes no clothes at all – their garments had been burnt by bombing or torn to make bandages for the wounded. Evacuees from the *Mata Hari*, however, had brought their suitcases into camp, except for Ruth Russell-Roberts, the lovely Hartnell model, whose suitcase was stolen on the Muntok pier.

The women became creative through necessity. Curtain fabric and nuns' habits were used to make brief shorts and halter tops. Pieces of wire from the fence around the camp were taken to use as knitting needles and woollen garments were unravelled and remade. Wood was shaped into rough sandals, called 'trompers', so women could walk through the foul mud and the latrine effluent that flooded in the torrential rain. The camp toilets comprised open drains with no running water. It was necessary for volunteers to scoop faeces from the drains into buckets with coconut shells, trying to reduce the stench and the risk of flies transmitting disease throughout the camp. The Australian nurses and other brave women performed this ghastly but necessary task.

Reverend Vic Wardle from the men's camp had brought some of his wife's and daughter's clothes with him on the *Mata Hari*, hoping to meet them somewhere on the journey. Instead, they were now in South Africa. He sent the dresses and items of his own to the women's camp. Elderly Mrs Mary Brown from the *Vyner Brooke* made herself a dress from the reverend's striped pyjamas. She created a sunhat from an old umbrella and made shady hats for others from bamboo and dried grass. Her shoes were large sailor's shoes found abandoned in Muntok Jail. Other women took sarongs from an abandoned house when they landed without clothing.

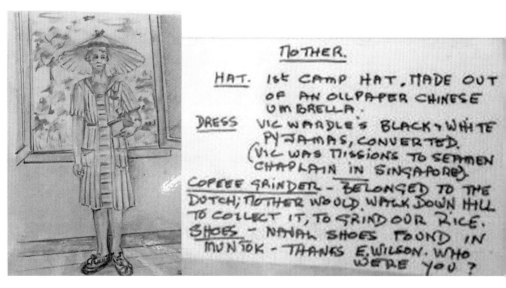

Resourceful Mrs Mary Brown.

PALEMBANG

Right: Sumatran houses, showing drains.

Below: Street drains used as latrines, Irenelaan, Palembang.

Charitas Hospital, Palembang 1942–43

Despite the prisoners' struggles to remain healthy, many became unwell, particularly with dysentery and malaria. In the first eighteen months of internment, the Japanese permitted some patients to be brought from the men's and women's civilian prison camps by truck to the nearby Charitas Catholic Hospital. Here the doctors and nursing nuns cared for the sick, keeping many in hospital longer than needed, to strengthen them and to reduce their risk of dying when they were returned to camp. Several prisoners died and were buried in the hospital grounds. A number of babies were born in Charitas Hospital during the first months of imprisonment.

In addition to providing much-needed care, the doctors and nuns scheduled medical appointments to allow husbands and wives to meet briefly in the hospital – this was often the first each knew the other was still alive. Patients returning to camp brought news of other patients and could sometimes smuggle medicines, messages and money given at the hospital. After the war, Australian nurse Mavis Hannah described how she had brought letters back to camp inside a sanitary pad worn next to her skin. In *A Nursing Sister's Account of Life as a Prisoner of the Japanese*, Mavis reports: 'I was eventually taken to the guard house, then to a house nearby where the Kempeitai [Japanese Gestapo or secret police] bullied me, hit me and tried to make me implicate others.'

One Charitas Hospital staff member was Dr Annamaria Eleanora Curth Goldberg, a German Jewish doctor who had been on the *Vyner Brooke*. Dr Goldberg and her psychiatrist husband, who is thought to have died in the evacuation from Singapore, had left Germany for Italy to escape Hitler. Later in Malaya, as Germans, they were deemed enemy aliens and experienced house arrest. In Charitas Hospital, Dr Goldberg cared for child internees Des Woodford, who had been hit in the eye, and Neal Hobbs, admitted with dysentery. Both later spoke very highly of her. The Australian nurses, however, were very critical of Dr Goldberg's behaviour and attitude in camp, saying she had favoured herself over patients' well-being. The nurses gave unfavourable details to the Australian Government after the war when Dr Goldberg applied to become an Australian citizen. Her application was rejected, and she returned to Singapore, later marrying Lord Charles Murray-Aynsley, the Singapore Chief Justice, in 1952.

Charitas Hospital was suddenly closed by the Japanese in 1943 when staff were accused of spying. Dr Ziesel and nine others were beheaded. Dr Tekelenburg was sent to a military prison at Soengeiliat on the East of Bangka Island, where he died. He was a surgeon and it was said that the Japanese had cut off his hands.

Charitas Hospital, Palembang, *c*.1935.

Reverend Mother Alocoque, the leader of the Charitas nuns, was also sent to a military prison, where she knelt praying and would not speak to her captors. The other nuns hid medicines under their habits before they were imprisoned in the Palembang women's camp. Here the forty nuns continued to care for the captive women and children. Four nuns died in the

PALEMBANG

camps from sickness and starvation. Mother Alocoque and her nuns later received a medal from England's King George VI after the war for their care of the prisoners. This medal is in the hospital museum today.

The hospital buildings were taken over by the Japanese in 1943 and used for military purposes. The hospital commands a clear view to the Moesi River.

Irenelaan Dutch Houses Women's Camp, Continued, 1 April 1942 to 20 September 1943

Meanwhile, long months passed in the women's camp, becoming a year and more. The physical condition of the women and children worsened from lack of food and medicine. Despite this, the prisoners tried to maintain their spirits.

Children played together or attended classes given by the women. The women met for afternoon tea with 'bring your own food', wrote down recipes from home (of course, not able to be created in camp but comforting to dream about) and placed bright jungle flowers in jars inside their crowded homes. They made birthday cards from improvised materials and gave one another gifts of tiny cakes made from hoarded ground rice and coconut.

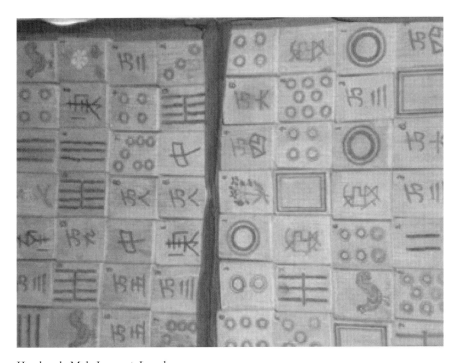

Handmade Mah-Jong set, Irenelaan camp.

THE EVACUATION OF SINGAPORE

Margaret Dryburgh, a Presbyterian missionary, wrote many poems and made little cards to cheer the women. Internee Shelagh Brown recalled how Miss Dryburgh would quietly 'slip a card or picture to a friend who was feeling low'. She also drew accurate pictures of the camp buildings, which remain to show the harsh living conditions.

The women tried to keep busy in spare time left after caring for their children and carrying out their many chores. They snipped pieces from clothing to make patchwork items and pulled coloured threads from their tattered clothes to create small embroideries, a few of which survive. A precious sewing needle was passed from person to person.

The backs of photos left behind in the Dutch houses were painted to make playing cards, and scraps of wood were smoothed and polished to form tiles for mah-jong sets. The women were not frivolous in these actions but hoped to distract themselves, their children and their friends from worry and hunger.

Above left: Embroidery made by Australian Army nurse Jean Ashton in camp. She pulled coloured threads from her clothes to sew the design.

Above middle: Rag doll made in camp by Mrs Mary Brown for her unborn grandchild. This doll and her granddaughter attended the Chichester Vocal Orchestra Concert in 2013.

Above right: 'Bully', Japanese doll made in camp by Australian Army nurse Betty Jeffrey as a gift for Vivian Bullwinkel.

Kami Hanya Minum Susu – We Only Drink Milk

Japanese soldiers tried to start an 'officers' club' in one of the Dutch camp houses, ordering women prisoners to work there. The women knew that a brothel rather than a simple club with drinks and dancing was planned. Four girls were requested to attend the club opening but the Australian Army nurses attended together. They dirtied their faces and clothes and coughed loudly, pretending to have TB

PALEMBANG

(tuberculosis) to discourage the soldiers' advances. They refused any alcohol, the nurses announcing that 'Australian girls only drink milk'. Fortunately, the women's actions succeeded and the plan for the 'officers' club' was abandoned.

Prisoners at Irenelaan (Incomplete List of Names)

After the war, former child internee Ralph Armstrong and internee Mamie Colley compiled lists of women and children who had lived in the Irenelaan camp. Only names they remembered are included here. The names of the many Dutch women and children were not always known to them. Some Eurasian prisoners were returned to Singapore and interned there and may not be recorded on this list. The former Dutch workers' houses in the camp were small and compact with three rooms, so we can see the enormous overcrowding that followed, adding to sanitation problems. By the end of the war, one third of all women prisoners and a number of children had died from disease and starvation in the Palembang, Muntok and Belalau camps.

House 1 Dutch women and children.

House 2 Mrs Bull and Hazel, Christine Bundy, Norah Chambers, Marguerite Carruthers, Mrs Daniels, Mrs Dixie, Mrs Dominicus, Sonia Geike, Mrs Gilmour, Grace Gurr, Mrs Hinch, Mrs Jennings, Mrs Kenneison and Betty, Mamie Mackintosh, Mrs MacLennan, Ena Murray, Audrey Owen, Mrs Plummer, Mrs Rodriguez, Ruth Russell-Roberts, Miss de Souza, Dr Smith, Mrs Self, Vi Stevens, Mrs Stevenson, Mrs Woodford and Desmond.

House 3 Mrs Leicester-Dunn, Percy and Maureen, Nurse Kong and others.

House 4 Miss Dixon, Miss Hartley, Mrs Ling with Norma and Peter, Mrs Macanlandish, Miss Mackinnon, Mrs Helen Mackenzie, Mrs Ivy Matthews, Mrs Netta Smith, Dr Thompson.

House 5 Mrs Battenby, Mrs L.J. Beeston, Miss Coupland, Mrs Coates, Mrs Cross, Mrs Hastings, Mrs Hennessey, Mrs Harding, Mrs Hilton, Dr MacDowell, Mrs Maddon, Mrs Mellor, Mrs Pugh, Mrs Skinner, Mrs Tilborne, Mrs van Buren, Miss van Buren, Miss van Geysel, Mrs Watters.

House 6 Dutch women and children, Mrs Cooke, Mrs Nailor, Mrs Thane and Pamela.

House 7 Australian Army nurses Pat Blake, Shirley Gardham, Mavis Hannah, Blanche Hempstead, Elizabeth Simons, Wilma Oram and others, Mrs Blake and Dennis, Mrs Close with John, David, Joan and Sheila, Mrs Dominguez, Miss Murray, Mrs McKechnie.

House 8 Australian Army nurses Sister James and others, British nurses Castle, MacCallum and Rossie, Miss Gilmour, Mrs Leyland, Mrs James, Mrs Phyllis Tunbridge, Mrs Ward.

THE EVACUATION OF SINGAPORE

House 9 Dutch women and children, Mrs Beeftink with Frieki and Janje, Mrs Grootes and Chris, Sister de Groote, Mrs de Radder (and dog), Miss Van der Lee, Mrs Shoonberger and Hans, Peter and Benny, Mrs Teklenberg with Katy and Elsje, Miss Sally Toppe.

Garage 9 Mrs Brown and Shelagh, Phyllis Briggs, Miss Cullen, Mrs Colley, Miss Dryburgh, Mary (Paddy) Glasgow, Mrs Jenkins, Miss Livingston, Miss Mackintosh, Mrs MacLeod, Sally Oldham, Eve Prouse, Agnes Weir, Misha Warman.

House 10 ?

House 11 Miss Angus, Mrs Resie Armstrong with Ralph and June Bourhill, Miss Dixie Armstrong, Mrs Bedell, Mrs Boswell with Drina, Joan, Maisie and Kenneth, Mrs Charlotte Boswell, Mrs Claire Boswell with Phyllis Ann, Mrs Chan and Johnnie, Mrs Day, Mrs Effort, Mrs Gooder, Mrs Paterson and Robbie, Mrs Simmonds, Mrs Grace Watters-Price with Sivo, Mrs Sinnatt with Anthony and baby Judith (born in camp).

Garage 11 Mrs Anderson, Mrs Austin, Mrs Frith, Mrs Hutchings, Mrs Langdon Williams, Mrs Tunn.

House 12 Miss Cooper, Nurse Dexter, Mrs Doris Frampton, Mrs Valda Godley, Mrs Gregory, Mrs Gray (tall), Mrs Grey (short), Mrs Laybourne, Mrs Lim,

Old house with shutters, Palembang.

PALEMBANG

Mrs Maddan, Mrs Maddams, Miss Dorothy Morton, Mrs Pennyfather, Mrs Powell, Mrs Pulford, Mrs Stranger, Mrs Molly Watts-Carter.

House 13 Granny Anthony, Mrs Barbara, Mrs Curran-Sharp, Mrs Jess, Mrs Jones, Mrs Holweg, Mrs MacAlister, Mrs McFie, Olga Neubronner, Miss Margot Turner, Dutch women.

House 14 Mrs Dyne with Harry, Mrs Gardiner, Miss Haines, Mrs Hepburn, Mrs Hilda Holderness, Mrs M James, Mrs Mabel Kennedy and baby, Mrs Doris Leyland, Miss Phyllis and ? Miss Doris Liddelow, Mrs M. James, Mrs Joyce Roberts, Mrs Zaida Short, Mrs Sinclair with Joan and Ian, Miss Lottie Wales, Mrs Ward, Mrs Van Geysel with Maureen, Jean, Joyce and Shirley.

House 15 Olive Bayliss, Mrs Gardiner, Mrs Gibson, Miss A. Haynes, Miss Hepburn, Mrs Ismail, Molly Ismail, Mrs Reid with James, Erica, Jane, Roy and Dirk and grandmother Mrs Kobus, Mrs Sammy, Mrs Phyllis Tunbridge.

House 16 Helen, Antoinette and Allette Colijn, Mrs Van den Haut, Mrs Muller and others.

House 17, Miss Corinth and others.

House 18 Reverend Mother Laurentia and nun.

Unknown houses, Susie Stevens and Christie, Iris Robinson, Pat Sandy, Daphne and Phyllis Schooling and Schooling child, Evelyn Parr and others.

Palembang Jail Men's Camp, April 1 1942 to 16 January 1943

The civilian male internees, meanwhile, strove to remain alive in Palembang Jail and at Pladjoe. The captives elected British and Dutch camp leaders and formed committees for cooking, washing and sanitation. As in the women's camp, food supplies were limited and lacking in nutrition. The men were issued with a handful of white rice for each meal – this was sometimes supplemented with a stale vegetable and a very occasional flake of meat.

A magazine, *Camp News,* was produced weekly for a number of months while the men's strength and paper lasted. It was edited and typed by American Journalist William McDougall and fellow internee William Probyn Allen. Four copies of the magazine, two in English and two in Dutch, with coloured illustrations, circulated among the 480 men. The magazines were read quickly and passed on to other readers. Articles about camp activities, details of church services, gossip, recipes and humour were included, aiming to inform, entertain and help while away the long, dreary hours. A few possessions were offered for sale, and a general knowledge quiz offered first prize of a precious fried egg. An advertisement called for old clothes to be used for dysentery rags.

THE EVACUATION OF SINGAPORE

The men tried to fill their days with lectures, foreign language and music lessons, concerts and a badminton match. *Camp News* describes several concerts held in the first months, with clever skits and costumes. These songs, sketches and ditties all helped to distract the internees from their otherwise grim and hungry lives. Coconut shells worn on the chest aided the semblance of women's costumes and raised a needed laugh. Donald Pratt was one concert member much appreciated by the audience. In real life, he was the nephew of Hollywood horror actor Boris Karloff (who was born as William Henry Pratt).

Later, when the men were sent back to Muntok, William McDougall buried the pages of his diary and *Camp News* in bottles and cans along the foundations of a camp building. A pipe was laid as a ruse to deceive the Japanese. He retrieved the intact pages from their hiding place at the end of the war.

Words of the poem 'Say Not the Struggle Nought Availeth', by Arthur Hugh Clough, were published in one edition of *Camp News*. This poem had been popularized in a wartime speech by Winston Churchill, and the stanza must have encouraged the internees to hope for better times. The poem was set to music by Muntok's interned priest, Father Bakker. It was his dying wish that the song should be given to Dutch Queen Wilhelmina and to Winston Churchill after the war and this indeed took place. The words 'by eastern windows' from this poem formed the title of William McDougall's post-war book about the men's camp.

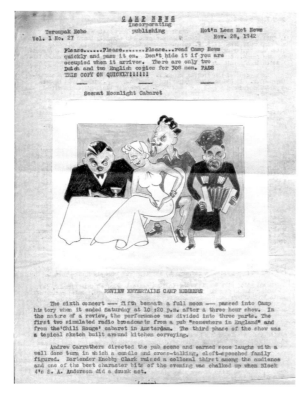

A hand-coloured page of *Camp News* describing a moonlight cabaret concert held by the men in Palembang Jail, November 1942.

PALEMBANG

Hunting rats for dinner in Chung Wa Palembang men's military camp, drawn by Lieutenant William Bourke, Royal New Zealand Navy, Prisoner of War, Muntok and Palembang.

Cooking in camp, drawn by Lieutenant William Bourke, Royal New Zealand Navy, Prisoner of War, Muntok and Palembang.

Palembang Jail became more overcrowded as extra prisoners were brought in. The Japanese ordered the men to build themselves a new camp at Poentjak Sekoening ('Yellow Peak', named after the surrounding trees with yellow blooms). This area was half an hour's walk from the jail, in an open field close to the women's Dutch Houses Camp. For several months, a group of fifty men walked from the jail each day to work on the new site.

Many men asked to join the work party to experience the freedom of being outside the high jail walls. The walk also provided exercise, the opportunity to barter with local people for much-needed food and to pass near the women's camp. The men laboured with local workers to build the new camp huts made from bamboo and atap (thatch made from palm leaf). The finished camp would be surrounded by a barbed-wire fence, with Japanese and Korean guards.

As the working party passed near the women's houses each day, the women climbed onto a high wall and waved and called to the men. They were too far away to speak but at least could recognise one another and know that their loved ones were still alive.

Christmas 1942

On Christmas Eve 1942, as the men's work party neared the women standing on the wall, there was no sound. The waiting women were still. The men paused, worried that something was wrong.

Suddenly women's voices arose, singing 'O Come All Ye Faithful' and then 'Silent Night'. The men listened in silence, with overflowing hearts. Even the guards were moved by the music and, instead of shouting and beating the men, allowed them to walk past slowly.

On Boxing Day, the men's camp choir joined the working party, led by Father Bakker. As they reached the wall, the men reciprocated by singing carols to the waiting women. The guards would not allow the men to stop, but they walked past the women as slowly as possible, reaching out to their wives, children and friends with their heartfelt gift of song.

On Christmas Day, the internees held church services in English and Dutch. Carefully hoarded ingredients were used to make a special meal, and small gifts were exchanged. The women made toffee from hard palm sugar and sent pieces to male internees who had no wives or children in the women's camp.

At great risk, internee Anton Colijn arranged to meet his three daughters secretly in the wasteland near the women's camp. He gave them a cooked chicken he had bargained for and all his love. This was the last time they would ever meet – he died in Muntok Men's Camp on 11 March 1945. Colijn was the son of a past Dutch prime minister. He and his daughters had been shipwrecked with William McDougall before entering the camps – the girls sent McDougall a wallet they had made and embroidered with his initials as a Christmas gift.

PALEMBANG

William Probyn Allen, the co-editor of *Camp News*, wrote the following poem dedicated to his wife at Christmas 1942, remembering their past together and with hopes for the future. Sadly, they were not able to meet again. He died on 25 March 1945 at Belalau men's civilian camp at Loeboek Linggau, Sumatra.

To My Wife at Christmas
It needs no festal time to bring you to my mind,
for every sunrise, every close of day, I find
your image by me, smiling, bidding me good cheer,
whispering our private nonsenses I love to hear.
Yet to be parted at this season, for this cause,
Seems doubly hard to bear, though if men break the laws
Of Him on high, they have only themselves to blame
for suffering; the Eternal Rules are still the same.
Last year I hung a stocking, childlike, by your bed
While you were sleeping, but this year my thoughts instead,
And prayers and wishes to the stars and round moon spoken,
Are all the gifts that I can send to you for token
Of all the joy there is between us, come what may.
Have faith, my love, although the night is dark, the day
will break and peace and good will come to men at last.
God bless and keep you always.

Men's Barracks Camp, Palembang, 16 January 1943 to 19 September 1943

The bamboo and palm leaf camp huts built by the men were completed in January 1943. The men left Palembang Jail to move into their new prison camp, carrying their meagre possessions and anything else they had managed to scrounge. They were no longer confined by stone walls but there were many new problems. They were joined by 200 more Dutch internees, and the camp became extra crowded. Torrential rain fell through the palm leaf roofs. In the downpours, the open drains used as latrines flooded the earth floors of the huts, swilling over the men's feet. Rats and lice lived in the roughly hewn roofs and walls, plaguing the prisoners at night. They developed sores and rashes from insect bites and could not sleep.

There was inadequate food and sanitation, and their situation was worsened by a shortage of fresh water. The men dug a deep well for drinking – the water was brown and muddy and needed to be boiled. This meant that extra wood must be chopped for the fire, depleting their energy reserves. Water was rationed and sticky mud was everywhere. Bathing was limited and hygiene compromised, leading to skin infection and frequent dysentery.

The men continued to hope the war would end soon or that they would be repatriated home in exchange for Japanese prisoners. But this was not to be.

THE EVACUATION OF SINGAPORE

In September 1943, the men were informed they were about to leave the atap barracks camp but were not told their destination. Believing their captors were going to live in the huts, the prisoners caused what damage they could and flung logs and rubbish into the well.

But the men were returned on barges down the Moesi River to the dreaded Muntok Jail on Bangka Island. The new inhabitants in the Palembang barracks camp were the civilian women prisoners from the nearby Dutch houses. The women's conditions had been cramped before, but they were now dismayed to find their new camp not only primitive and unhealthy but in a state of disrepair.

An attempt at a vegetable garden. The prisoners were moved before the vegetables were ready.

Palembang atap camp kitchen. Camp built by men and lived in first by men and later by women prisoners. The unusual forked trees still grow in this area (drawn by Margaret Dryburgh).

On Severed Wings

But let us join the night with severed wings!
Clear our lowly heartfelt fears
Golden wings joining ancient choirs
Soaring yonder, gilded flyers

Eira Day, daughter of child internee
Harry Dyne

Only the singing will ignite our spirits.

Internee Gordon Reis

The Palembang Prison Camp Women's Vocal Orchestra First Concert, 27 December 1943

The women were dispirited, far from home, hungry and ill. In an attempt to help morale, two English women internees, Norah Chambers and Margaret Dryburgh, both trained in classical music, began to form a camp choir. Norah and Margaret transcribed many pieces of classical music from memory. They then taught women of twenty different nationalities to sing the music without words, as a vocal orchestra. The women rehearsed in secret, each small part practised separately, as the Japanese forbade gatherings.

The first concert was held outside in the grounds of the palm leaf and bamboo camp on the evening of 27 December 1943. The audience was invited to attend and slowly came forward. The women were afraid of the guards but were excited at the prospect of something new. They tried to dress in something other than their usual worn and patched clothes. Some women had a dress put aside for a special occasion – or for liberation. Others shared a prized lipstick and little girls might have a coloured ribbon in their hair.

The choir entered slowly, carrying small stools as they were too weak to stand for the performance. The audience moved forward to listen. At first, the guards were angry, but as the first strains of music were heard, even they, usually harsh and bullying, were quiet. The strains of remembered and much-loved tunes gradually rose above the spellbound internees. It was the first beauty the women had experienced in nearly two years in the camp.

THE EVACUATION OF SINGAPORE

The programme included pieces by Bach, Beethoven, Chopin, Dvorak and Schubert – works recalled exactly by Norah and Margaret and carefully taught to the choir. Norah said afterwards that: 'Only six of our thirty women could read music – some pieces were learned note by note and line by line, which was a tremendous achievement by all.'

The audience sat motionless beneath the darkening skies, absorbing the wonderful sound. Their thoughts were lifted far above their hunger, their fear and loneliness, beyond the filth, sickness and odours as they remembered the peace, order and beauty of their past lives.

These women were starved and unwell and far removed from their normal living. They were humiliated and ill-treated, they were made to stand for long hours in the hot sun for roll calls and abused and beaten by their captors. They were afraid for their children and for their absent husbands. Despite all these hardships, the uplifting music gave the women the opportunity to find beauty and to escape into their imagination. Long after the last notes had finished, the women were moved and inspired by their experience.

The memory of the music stayed with the women during the months and years to come. Other concerts followed with the same wonderful effect until the choir became too weak to continue and death depleted their numbers. Shelagh Brown, later Mrs Shelagh Lea, recalled that three things helped her to endure life in prison camp – her faith in God, watching the colourful sunrise and sunset, which gave hope that life was ongoing, and singing the transcending music of the choir.

Day-to-day life in camp was difficult and demoralizing and at times dreadful. Always trying to help her fellow internees, Missionary Margaret Dryburgh wrote 'The Captives Hymn', which was sung at camp church services on Sundays:

Orchestra practice in the Dutch kitchen, drawn by Australian Army nurse Betty Jeffrey.

ON SEVERED WINGS

Father, in captivity,
We would lift our prayers to Thee,
Keep us ever in Thy love,
Grant that daily we may prove
Those who place their trust in Thee
More than conquerors may be.

Give us patience to endure,
Keep our hearts serene and pure,
Grant us courage, charity,
Greater faith, humility,
Readiness to own Thy will,
Be we free or captives still.

For our country we would pray,
In this hour be Thou her stay,
Pride and sinfulness forgive,
Teach her by Thy laws to live,
By Thy grace may all men see
That true greatness comes from Thee.

For our loved ones we would pray,
Be their guardian night and day,
From all danger keep them free,
Banish all anxiety.
May they trust us to Thy care,
Know that Thou our pains dost share.

May the day of freedom dawn,
Peace and justice be reborn,
Grant that nations loving Thee
O'er the world may brothers be,
Cleansed by suffering, know rebirth,
See Thy kingdom come on earth.

The words of the lovely hymn gave comfort and support to the women prisoners. It is still sung in churches and by groups valuing freedom today.

Part of the music score of 'The Captives' Hymn'.

Where is My Cat?

When I recovered, I asked, 'Where is my cat?'
Father Elling said, 'You've eaten it.'
                         Ralph Armstrong, former child internee,
                                A Short Cruise on the Vyner Brooke

Muntok Jail Men's Camp, 19 September 1943 to 12 March 1945

The men prisoners, meanwhile, had been taken from the bamboo and palm-leaf camp they built in Palembang and driven, standing in trucks, to the Moesi River. Here they were herded into barges. They travelled along the familiar route down the wide, brown river – hungry and cramped, a journey of many hours. Eventually,

Concrete sleeping platforms where many men lay side by side.

they reached the open sea of the Bangka Strait, where so many had been bombed in February 1942. The ocean was no longer a battlefield but was now calm, and the air fresh and clean. The men were hopeful and wished their destination might be Singapore, Java or even Australia.

Alas, the barges did not change course but proceeded across the Strait to Bangka Island. The men landed at the 600m-long Muntok pier and were marched through the town to the grim, foreboding gates of the Muntok Jail. Hearts sank at the memory of the harsh time already spent here.

Originally built to house 200 native prisoners, now 639 men were crammed inside. Some 960 were later imprisoned in the jail as more internees were brought from other sites. Once more, the men slept crushed together on the sloping concrete slabs like fish for sale in a market. Unlike a market, though, there were no fish to eat, only ever-decreasing measures of vitamin-poor white rice with a few strings of decaying vegetables and a rare tiny shred of meat.

Sometimes the only food was a small bowl of overcooked, watery rice like glue. This was nicknamed 'ongle-ongle' and had no taste at all. If not eaten, it formed a useful paste to help treat deep tropical leg ulcers.

Sickness and Starvation – Muntok Men's and Women's Camps

The human race is sustained by kindness, friendship and hope but underpinning these is a fundamental need for good nutrition. The prisoners tried to care for and support one another and to provide extra food to the sick where possible but inadequate food was provided. Without proper requirements of calories, carbohydrates, fats, proteins and vitamins and clean water, health could not be maintained and serious diseases developed. Medicines to treat these were absent or in very short supply.

Vitamin B1 (thiamine) deficiency, exacerbated by eating husked white rice rather than brown rice, developed in many internees, causing beriberi. This was of two forms – dry and wet. Dry beriberi affected the function of physical nerves so that victims lost the ability to walk or to see. Wet beriberi caused fluid to build up in the limbs, the abdomen, the lungs and around the heart. Arms and legs swelled like tree trunks and the patients became unable to breathe, drowning in their own congestion. Prisoners caring for patients with wet beriberi heard their characteristic noisy, laboured breathing before death, which was known as the 'beriberi song'.

In addition to beriberi, extreme lack of Vitamin B1 also led to cerebral changes of Wernicke's and Korsakoff's encephalopathy, leading to memory loss, psychosis and dementia.

Beriberi was first identified 4,500 years ago in China. It was well-known in Asia, where white rice was a staple food; it was a therefore a condition that was well-understood by the Japanese. Despite this awareness, brown rice, soy beans or other vitamin B1-containing foods were not provided to the prisoners, with terrible consequences.

Lack of Vitamin B3 in the diet (niacin), found in grains and meat, was a cause of pellagra, with skin rashes and psychiatric symptoms. Together with brain changes from lack of thiamine, pellagra is likely to have caused some prisoners to become very disturbed and attempt or commit suicide.

Vitamin C, iron and zinc deficiency contributed to many skin disorders. Poor nutrition, together with infected insect bites, led to deep leg ulcers often eroding to the bone. Lack of medical supplies meant these could only be treated with salt water applications or rice paste. If very severe, the ulcers sometimes led to limb amputation.

Infectious dysentery, with frequent watery and blood-stained diarrhoea, also afflicted the captives, robbing them of fluids and nutrition, leading to exhaustion, collapse and death.

Bangka Island was then and is still a malarial area, transmitted by mosquito bites. Without mosquito nets to prevent bites or quinine tablets for prevention and treatment, the men began to suffer recurrent episodes. Some contracted the usually fatal cerebral malaria – a few, including William McDougall, were very lucky to survive this. Young Des Woodford recovered after a prolonged malarial episode to find he had been helped back to health by eating soup made from his pet cat. Deadly attacks of 'Bangka fever' (possibly dengue fever) also took their toll on the weakened and malnourished prisoners and was a frequent cause of death in the Muntok camps.

The Tinwinning 'Hospital', 19 September 1943 to 12 March 1945

Critically ill and dying men were moved from Muntok Jail into the Tinwinning 'hospital' building connected to the jail by a barbed wire walkway. There were no beds for these sick and dying men – they lay shoulder to shoulder on concrete slabs or, if fortunate, on a ragged sack.

Here, although there were no medicines available, the men were able to lie still, cared for by their fellow captives. The 'hospital' staff spoon-fed the patients rice gruel and carried bedpans back and forwards to the dysentery sufferers. McDougall commented on the nonstop clatter of the metal pans.

A large number of Catholic brothers were interned in the jail, together with Bishop Mekkelholt of Palembang and Muntok's priest, Father Bakker. The brothers were among those who volunteered to nurse the dying men, making a special request that they care for the dysentery victims. Eleven brothers became ill and died due to this dedicated work in Muntok. Father Bakker later died in Belalau camp.

Death generally claimed the Tinwinning 'hospital' patients, who could have lived with food, medicines and proper hospital care.

The jail was overcrowded, but additional prisoners were brought in from prison camps at Pangkal Pinang to the east of Bangka Island and from Benkoelen in

WHERE IS MY CAT?

Sumatra. Soon nearly 1,000 men were crammed into the Muntok Jail and 'hospital' wards. The Japanese kept registration cards for the prisoners and deaths were carefully recorded – the Japanese gave internee William McDougall a typewriter and required him to compile lists of the dead. We know that 270 Dutch, British, Australian and New Zealand civilian men died in Muntok Camp during this eighteen-month period.

The Japanese, who had not helped the men while they lived, allowed them to hold funerals. Rough bamboo coffins lay waiting each day. Taller people were bent to fit inside the boxes, and fluid from bodies swollen with beriberi leaked from the slats. As deaths increased, the top and sides of the coffins were reused and the dead buried on a plank or, as time progressed, wrapped in a cloth. While they had strength, their friends carried each body a mile up the hill and through the town to the Muntok civil cemetery, also known as the town or 'old Dutch' cemetery, where they dug graves for the deceased.

Astonishingly, the camp commandant, Captain Seiki Kazue, donated wreaths for the funerals, although the money would have been much better used for food and medicines for the living. The mourners held a brief service, said prayers and sang the hymn 'Abide with Me'. The men's friends marked the graves with rough wooden crosses, and the location of each plot was carefully recorded. The men then walked slowly back along the treed boulevard to the jail.

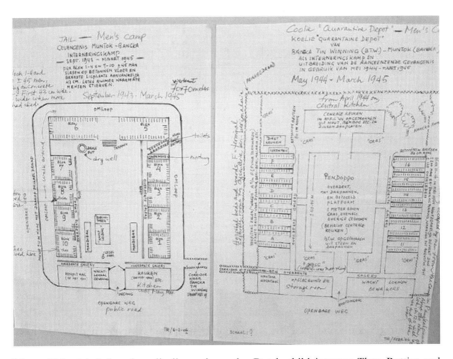

Map of Muntok Jail and coolie lines, drawn by Dutch child internee Theo Rottier and reproduced with his permission.

THE EVACUATION OF SINGAPORE

My grandfather died in Muntok Jail on 2 August 1944 from dysentery and beriberi. He was 53 years old. His effects were returned to my grandmother after the war and included his wedding ring and £19. Although this sounds like a fair sum of money, it would only have brought a few eggs at inflated prices from the black-market traders.

Above: Muntok Jail, men's camp.

Left: Men in the Muntok Jail.

WHERE IS MY CAT?

Teenage Boys Sent from Palembang to Muntok Jail, 1943–44

The civilian women and child prisoners were held in the atap huts in Palembang for many months, together with the nurses and forty nuns from the Charitas Hospital. In an attempt to improve their poor rations, they tried to grow vegetables from seeds saved from their cooking. The vegetable patches were fertilised by faeces they collected from the drains. But the prisoners were later moved back to Muntok before the vegetables were ready.

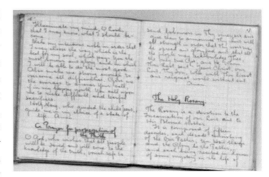

Prayer book made for Ralph Armstrong, 'O God, who wishes that all people will be saved, make me strong enough to overcome all difficulties'.

The women tried hard to care for their children, coaxing them to eat the decaying and sparse food and struggling to clothe them. They attempted to teach the children, who preferred to play simple games in the dirt with sticks and stones until they became too weak and lethargic.

On a number of occasions, Japanese camp leader Captain Seiki Kazue ordered all growing boys in the Palembang women's prison camp to assemble, face him and pull down their pants. In this way, he judged which boys had started puberty. These young boys were told to say farewell to their mothers immediately and were sent away to the men's camp in Muntok that same day, perhaps so they could not challenge the guards as they grew. The women and the boys were distraught – they had no idea where the boys were going, whether male relatives were still alive and if mothers and sons would ever meet again.

The boys were taken in trucks to the Moesi River and sent on boats to the Muntok Jail. Some boys re-joined their fathers, but those without a relative in camp were allocated a male guardian from among the internees. If the guardian died, another man was chosen to oversee the boy's welfare. It was a harsh upbringing for boys only 12 or 13 years old.

The Catholic priests and brothers tried to educate the boys, making prayer books from scrap paper. Some boys were confirmed in camp.

Women and Young Children Return to Muntok, 3 October 1944 to 16 April 1945

In October 1944, the women and younger children were removed from the Palembang atap barracks camp. They were sent in groups over several days, once more in cramped boats along the Moesi River to Muntok. On reaching Bangka

THE EVACUATION OF SINGAPORE

Island after many hours, they were left overnight on the long Muntok pier with no food or facilities. The next day they were taken to a new bamboo and atap prison camp ringed by barbed wire. They were placed here, a few kilometres away from their husbands and sons confined in Muntok Jail – neither knowing that their loved ones were there.

At first the women felt this camp was an improvement over Palembang – the huts were newly built and clean, and a cool breeze blew through the trees. But the poor rations continued, and the preceding two years of increasing starvation and weakness had affected them all. Beriberi, dysentery, malaria, TB and tropical ulcers continued, and now the fatal Bangka fever added to the toll.

The doctors, nurses, nuns and volunteers tried to care for the sick women and children in a 'hospital' hut in the camp. The patients were sponged with cool cloths and offered sips of liquid but without medicine or facilities, little other help could be offered. Seventy-six women died in Muntok Camp, including two Australian Army nurses and four Catholic nuns. They were buried under rubber trees at the edge of the camp in shallow graves dug by their friends. The children helped to build the coffins, and names were burnt into rough wooden crosses with a poker.

Left: Muntok Women's Camp 'hospital 'hut and cemetery among rubber trees, drawn by internee and missionary Margaret Dryburgh.

Below: Block 5, Muntok Women's Camp, drawn by Margaret Dryburgh.

WHERE IS MY CAT?

The dying women often made a will, leaving their meagre possessions – a threadbare dress, patched blanket or broken comb – to their close friends. Without a will, their possessions automatically became the property of the Japanese Army.

Unlike the men, who were enclosed in the concrete compound of Muntok Jail, the women were surrounded by a wire fence. Some crept out at night to take food offerings from graves in the local Chinese cemetery. Women who still had any possessions left tried to barter with local people brave enough to approach the wire fence at night. In this way, an engagement or wedding ring could be exchanged for a few quinine tablets to treat malaria or a handful of Vitamin B-rich, lifesaving dried beans to help the severe symptoms of beriberi.

The penalties for trading were harsh. Prisoners were made to kneel in the hot sun for hours without shade or water. Some local traders were punished severely and were not seen again, believed to have been executed.

Belalau Men's and Women's Camps, Loeboek Linggau, Sumatra, 1 March 1945 (Men) and 8 April 1945 (Women) to October 1945

When it seemed that life could become no worse, the Japanese moved the captives yet again. They were taken back across the Bangka Strait and along the Moesi River to Palembang. From here they were transported by train and truck to their final camp at Belalau, near Loeboek Linggau, a mountainous region near Lahat in Western Sumatra. The men were moved in March and the women in April 1945. Some men were too ill to travel and remained in Muntok Jail with interned Dutch Dr Lentze and an orderly to care for them. All but four of these sick men died and were buried in Muntok.

The journey to Palembang was dreadful, lasting two nights and a day in the cramped and stifling barges. Friends carried the sickest women to the Muntok pier as the women did not trust the Japanese to care for them if they were left behind. One lady died as they left Muntok and was buried at sea. In Palembang, the prisoners were placed into closed railway trucks, out of sight of local people, and taken to Loeboek Linggau. A further seven women died on this terrible journey.

Their destination was Belalau, an abandoned rubber plantation in the mountains 10 miles north of Loeboek Linggau. The overgrown plantation and jungle were so dense and the area so isolated that the prisoners became afraid for the first time. They felt they would never be found and believed that this seclusion was deliberate.

The men and women were placed in separate camps but did not know that the others were nearby – they were not even told when a child or husband or wife lay dying. Accommodation was in dirty, rat-infested huts that in better days had housed the rubber estate workers. A stream ran through the camps, providing drinking and washing water, although this soon became contaminated through bathing and effluent. There was very little food provided – the prisoners tried to supplement their diet with snails, rats and snake. The sickness and death rates were very high.

THE EVACUATION OF SINGAPORE

Although very weak and frail, the Australian Army nurses, their English, Dutch and Eurasian colleagues and other volunteers tried to care for sick women and children. In reality, there was little they could do for patients apart from trying to keep them comfortable. Records show that ninety-nine men and eighty-nine women, including two further Australian Army nurses and Muntok's Catholic priest Father Bakker, died and were buried at Belalau.

One of the male internees who died at Belalau was Dr Albert McKern, a much-loved Australian family doctor and obstetrician who had lived and worked in Penang in Malaya. Dr McKern had cared for many pregnant women and helped to deliver their babies safely. Now he was suffering from malaria and amoebic dysentery. Realising he was near death, he asked for a pencil and paper to make his will. He was very weak and unable to sit, but he could write and his mind was clear.

In this document, handwritten on a small scrap of paper, he asked that all his assets be realised in the future, when his wife and children had all died, and after several more years had passed. Dr McKern requested that all of the funds be then divided equally between his three universities of Sydney, Edinburgh and Yale, to be used for research into safer childbirth.

Dr Albert McKern died in Belalau Men's Camp on 16 June 1945. In due course, his final wishes were carried out. In 2008, AUS $12 million was distributed to help develop improved obstetric care – a wonderful legacy from a man trying to help others in the future while lying on his own terrible deathbed. He is much revered; people in Penang believe they still see the good doctor walking on the beach at night. We don't often think of a happy ghost, but I am sure Dr McKern would be one, glad to know that despite his death, women and children around the world have an improved chance of a healthier life.

Above left: Dr Albert Stanley McKern.

Above right: Stream in dense jungle, Belalau camp site, Lubuk Linggau, Sumatra.

WHERE IS MY CAT?

Belalau men's and women's camps were guarded but were surrounded by tangles of barbed wire. A few internees risked the patrolling guards to slip under the wire and through a drain at night to leave the camp and forage for food. They looked for ubi kayu (tapioca root) tubers, growing wild or in farmers' fields, to wrench from the ground and smuggle back to camp. The ubi could be cooked and eaten or sold to other prisoners.

The penalty if caught outside the camp was extreme – the culprits were beaten and locked in solitary confinement with reduced rations for up to a month. One man found outside the wire was taken away by the guards and was not seen by his friends again.

When food supplies were critical, one internee, a big game hunter, was allowed to hunt for food. He was given a rifle and, surrounded by armed Japanese, was permitted to shoot wild animals to supplement the camp rations. Once, a wild boar was killed and another time, a deer, but these did not go far among 600 men, especially when the Japanese guards took the choicest cuts. Another time, a monkey was shot and brought into camp, but the men found it difficult to cook and eat this creature that looked so nearly human.

Over

My Mother, Dixie and Grace were all gone and I would never see them again.

Ralph Armstrong, former child internee,
A Short Cruise on the Vyner Brooke

'Now we can all be friends', Belalau, 24 August 1945

Life and death continued in this way until 24 August 1945. On this day, Captain Seiki Kazue called the men and the women together in their respective camps. The prisoners thought he was gathering them to stand before him so the guards could kill them all. This was not an unrealistic fear, as it was believed that the Japanese had been given orders for all prisoners to be executed if they were losing the war.

Instead, Captain Seiki stood on a table in each camp and addressed the crowd, 'The war is over,' he said. 'Now we can be friends.' He did not announce who had won the war. The prisoners did not celebrate but stood numbly and many cried.

Internee John (Jock) Cowie Brodie wrote of the liberation in his memoirs:

> On the day before the declaration of peace by the Jap commandant – who of course did not admit defeat – a sudden and unexpected increase amounting to 100% in the camp rations took place. It was generally anticipated that some very important events had occurred to force such a change.

The new and destructive atomic bombs had been dropped on Hiroshima and Nagasaki on 6 and 9 August 1945, and Japan's Emperor Hirohito had broadcast Japan's surrender on the radio on 15 August. The prisoners at Belalau did not learn of the surrender until nine days later, and the camps were not completely emptied until 7 October.

Belalau men's and women's camps were among the very last to be liberated in Sumatra. The Japanese repeatedly denied their existence, fearing repercussions when the skeletal prisoners were found and the high death rate known.

Major William Alston Tebbutt, who had been in charge of the Australian Army nurses on the *Vyner Brooke*, had been in Muntok Jail in February 1942. Here he learned of the massacre on Radji Beach, reported by sole nurse survivor Vivian

OVER

Bullwinkel. Major Tebbutt was later sent to Palembang and Changi prisoner of war camps, but, throughout the war, he had sought details of the nurses' location from soldiers who may have heard of them.

At the end of the war, Major Tebbutt insisted to Allied authorities that there must be further nurses held somewhere in Sumatra. After persistent questioning, the Japanese finally revealed that there *were* captives held at the abandoned rubber estate of Belalau, at Loeboek Linggau.

On 5 and 7 September 1945, Allied paratroopers Major G.F. Jacobs and Sergeant Major C.B. Hakkenberg entered Belalau men's and women's camps.

They had been parachuted into Sumatra to locate groups of prisoners and to ensure the Japanese camp commandants did not kill the captives or conceal their existence once the war had ended. Jacobs and Hakkenberg informed the Allied authorities of finding the captives at Belalau. On 13 September, food and newspapers were dropped into the camps and plans made to remove the prisoners to Palembang and Singapore. The liberation of the Sumatran camps is told in Gideon Jacobs' book, *Prelude to the Monsoon*.

The Sumatran prison camps were described as the worst in the East Indies. The prisoners 'looked like grey ghosts and women of 30 looked more like 100 years old'. Duncan Robertson wrote that survivors in Loeboek Linggau after the war were 'little more than walking skeletons'. He could almost close one hand around his thigh.

The captives were suddenly provided with Red Cross food parcels that had been hoarded in camp by the Japanese for years. Clothing, tinned food, mosquito nets and medicines materialised from the Japanese stores, useful but far too late for many. Duncan Robertson stated in his report to his employers after the war that:

> A few days later we were inundated with supplies of tinned foods consisting of meat, fish and Australian butter. The latter must have been 3½ years old but was in excellent condition. We also received 2 sets of Jap uniforms per man, boots, blankets and underclothing from their stocks. We bartered the clothing with natives from the kampongs for chickens and ducks as very few of us liked the idea of wearing a Jap uniform. It was almost incredible that a short time previously some of the internees had been eating rats, frogs, banana skins etc.

He continued:

> [T]he restriction of food was definitely a deliberate policy of the Japanese to bring about the deaths of all internees in the course of time – deaths were attributed to fever, Beriberi, etc but in actual fact the major cause of every one was malnutrition. There was plenty of food in this area, as proved by the production of chickens, ducks, eggs, beans and other foodstuffs immediately the armistice was announced on August 24 1945.

THE EVACUATION OF SINGAPORE

The delays in liberation following Japanese denial of the camps proved fatal for some prisoners. BBC Radio Broadcaster Andrew Carruthers died on 9 September 1945, still at Belalau Camp. He was able to be visited by his wife Marguerite, who had been in the women's camp, but he was critically ill and could not survive in the camp. Molly (Millicent) Watts-Carter also died in Belalau Camp after the war's end. She had lived through the bombings of both the Kuala and the Tanjong Pinang and the hardships of the camps but her strength finally failed. Australian Army nurse Pearl Mittelheuser also died in Belalau Camp after the surrender.

Some prisoners only learned of their families' deaths when they walked to find them in the nearby men's or women's camps. When one teenager who had been transferred to the men's camp as a boy visited the women's camp to find his family, he asked his little nephew where his own mother and two adult sisters were. The older boy learned that all three women, including the little boy's mother, had died.

Captain Annie Sage of the Royal Australian Nursing Service flew from Australia to Lahat to meet her nurses. She had brought sixty-five lipsticks. On seeing the emaciated group of twenty-four of the original sixty-five who had boarded the *Vyner Brooke* in Singapore in 1942, she asked where the other nurses were – 'This is all,' she was told. 'The others are dead.'

On 17 September, an aeroplane left Lahat for Singapore, carrying the twenty-four Australian Army nurses and thirty-six of the sickest women to hospital. Other internees were evacuated later and Belalau camps were emptied by 7 October. The prisoners had suffered three years and eight months of unbelievable hardship and over 500 of their fellows had died. The sickest survivors were taken to hospital and fed slowly so their bodies could become used to food again. Eating food too quickly after starvation could disturb the body's chemistry and be fatal.

In 1948, a war crimes tribunal in Medan sentenced Captain Seiki (Seki) Kazue to fifteen years' imprisonment for harsh treatment of the prisoners in these camps.

General Moritake Tanabe, the officer in charge of Sumatra, was sentenced to death. He denied ever having visited or knowing of the conditions in the prison camps.

Food drop into Belalau camp, 16 September 1945.

The Whole Horrible Episode

> Try and forget about the whole horrible episode. Think of it as a bad nightmare. You have all you need now and your freedom. Go out and enjoy yourselves[.]
>
> From a speech given by Lord Louis Mountbatten to PoWs and internees at Raffles Hotel, Singapore, September 1945

Life for the Survivors

On their release, military and civilian prisoners were handed leaflets informing them they must not discuss their prison camp experiences with families or the press. Some did not want to talk about the recent past but all were now unable to do so. There was no debriefing and very little support. The psychological effects of imprisonment were not well understood. Newspaper reports tell us that a doctor in Singapore caring for the Australian nurses released from Belalau remarked: 'They will go home as soon as we have fattened them up. A week will make a lot of difference. In a fortnight they will be themselves again.'

The Royal Australia Medical Corps major in charge of returned prisoners of war in Singapore in September 1945 commented:

> The health and morale of Australian prisoners of war from Japanese Camps are remarkably good. There is nothing wrong with the vast majority of men which good food, quiet and a quick return to normal life will not set right.

In an address to a Legacy luncheon in Perth, Dr K. Aberdeen stated:

> A primary rule which must be preached everywhere was that returned men must not be asked questions about their (wartime) experiences … Deformities, scars and crutches should be ignored as though they did not exist.

Others were more sympathetic, calling for help and understanding of returned prisoners and emphasizing there would be thousands of neurosis cases among prisoners of the Japanese. In the *Adelaide Advertiser* of 12 September 1945, Ian Sabey wrote of men and women released from camps where they had 'lived in perpetual anxiety – about their next meal, their next drop of water, their next hour'.

Brigadier Blackburn was quoted in the *News*, Adelaide on 22 September 1945 as saying:

> Nearly every man returning from prison camps in the Pacific is a neurosis case ... he had no knowledge of family, was always undernourished, always in an anxiety state, never knowing when he would be bashed, kicked or spat on [.]

Some efforts were made to understand the stress and trauma that PoWs and internees had undergone. Journalist Caroline Isaacson wrote in *The Melbourne Argus* on 28 August 1945:

> **Problem of the Prisoner of War when He is Home**
> It is the aftermath of War that often brings even greater problems than war itself and the problem now uppermost in my mind is that of the returned prisoner of war. Ever since our men were taken captive, many of us have shared their exile in our thoughts and in our hearts, but none of us at home could possibly have realised to the full all that they have had to endure. I know several returned POWs, and all are reluctant to speak of their experiences. It is not difficult, however, to piece together, from the little they will say, that cruelties and indignities of many years have left scars as deep in their minds as on their bodies. It is essential to keep that in mind, especially when the first excitement of his return home has passed, and it is important to remember that a man who has been a prisoner for a considerable time will be inclined to feel himself a stranger, not only in his home town but in his family circle.

Some prisoners were able to put the past behind them and resume their lives. A number returned to their occupations in Malaya and Singapore, while others settled in Australia, England, the Netherlands and South Africa. But many suffered what would be now recognised as post-traumatic stress disorder, with nightmares, anxiety and depression. As well as memories of individual suffering, the internees experienced sorrow and grief at the loss of family and friends from sickness and starvation in the prison camps. Some woke night after night, screaming. Many had disturbed family relationships or developed alcohol or medication dependence or long-term mental illness.

Many survivors report that they never spoke of their experiences, even when meeting fellow prisoners after the war. Some interned children were told by their parents to put the past behind them on their release and never think about it, as it was over and could not be changed.

THE WHOLE HORRIBLE EPISODE

The surviving Australian Army nurses returned home, to work or family life. Their story preceded them, with a torrent of newspaper articles describing the massacre at Radji Beach and the subsequent years of deprivation in the prison camps. Many families were unaware of their loved ones' fate for several months after the end of the war and must have thought the worst on reading about the nurses. My grandmother received a letter from Hal Hammett, the British leader of the men's camps, who wrote to all the bereaved families after the war:

> 4 May 1946
>
> Dear Mrs Campbell,
>
> It is, I am afraid, a long time since Colin died in August 1944. I gave all the details I could to the Australian representatives in Singapore after our release last September. And now I enclose the original Death Certificate, signed by Dr West and the sum of 19 pounds Australian currency, belonging to his estate.
>
> I did not know your husband before we met in Camp, but grew to know and like him in the close proximity of internment. He was always very cheery and took everything with a smile. It may comfort you to know that we suffered no active ill-treatment at the hands of the Japs. The story was rather one of general indifference and prolonged under-nourishment. And Colin was at least spared the last twelve months of anxious waiting.
>
> I shall be returning to Malaya very shortly, and if there is anything I can do for you, please do not hesitate to write to me.
>
> Yours very sincerely, H.G. Hammett

Melbourne Post-War

After the war, my grandmother remained in Melbourne with my father, who was now 20 years old and training to be an architect. Barney, her older son, returned from serving in the Middle East, married and moved to a home of his own.

My father and grandmother lived in a solid, red-brick flat in St Kilda. She and my grandfather had bought the block of flats to provide for their retirement, and now she managed the other tenants on her own. She enjoyed cooking, dressmaking and gardening – the pastimes she had not been able to pursue in her household run by servants in Malaya.

Her flat was neat and scrubbed clean with disinfectant and yellow soap. Asian ornaments sent ahead for the couple's planned life in Australia were displayed prominently. A black lacquer tray decorated with an orange bird and pomegranates stood in the fireplace, and carved wooden busts, a watercolour of a Malay man and a framed Eastern prayer adorned the mantelpiece. The poem

THE EVACUATION OF SINGAPORE

was titled 'Allah's Prayer' and showed a robed man with a camel, standing by a mosque:

> I pray the prayer the Easterns do, May the Peace of Allah abide with you.
> Wherever you stay, wherever you go, May the beautiful palms of Allah grow.
> Through the days of labour and nights of rest, May the love of sweet Allah make you blest.
> So I touch my heart as the Easterns do,
> May the Peace of Allah abide with you.

My grandmother was a Roman Catholic, but perhaps after living in the East and enduring her wartime experiences, she turned to all sources to help and comfort her.

She dealt with stress and memories by becoming active. An avid gardener, she trimmed and shaped the roses and hydrangeas in her neat garden beds with a fury. She flung soapy dish water on the bushes to kill aphids and wrenched small daisies and clover from the lawn. She quarrelled with her tenants who did not disinfect their rubbish bins. In these ways, she perhaps hoped to bring a measure of control back into the chaos that had swamped her life.

It was not unusual for women to be widowed and many had lost their husbands fighting in the war, but her husband's end had been so different – he was missing, first thought to have drowned and then, following his postcard, was believed to be safe. Instead, he had slowly and relentlessly starved, sickened and succumbed as a Japanese internee.

Many years later, when my grandmother had died, we emptied her flat. Her Edwardian dressing table held a bevelled, tri-fold mirror. The repeated, never-ending, scintillating images may have reminded her of those in the bedroom mirror once shattered by Bud the monkey in Malaya. A large carved box held the skin of

My grandmother, Anne Campbell, with sons John, in school cadet uniform, and Barney (Colin), Melbourne.

the legendary snake shot from under her by her husband. All their life's plans had been interrupted, and the skin had never been made into shoes or a handbag. Her fox fur stole, with its harsh glass eyes, yellow teeth and limp feet, hung in the camphor-reeking wardrobe.

The most telling surprise was when a large sum of money fluttered down from behind a painting on the wall – still more notes were found concealed in the chimney. I believe my grandmother was preparing for another war or evacuation, having lived with this possibility for the rest of her life.

My father studied, worked and married. When I was young, he did not talk of his own father, except once to say he had loved him more than anyone in the world. I am sure he did not speak about him to other people while he was growing up. It was an era when psychology was poorly understood and emotional pain was seen as a weakness. I knew my father as handsome, clever, artistic, humorous and kind, but, looking back, I can see he carried an oppressive burden. He suffered from what became known as the 'black dog', heavy and dark periods of his mood, increasingly frequent and debilitating. Ironically, the phrase 'black dog' was first coined to describe Winston Churchill's deep depression – it was Churchill who had minimised the Japanese threat to Malaya and Singapore, encouraging the British and Australians to remain before the war, rather than leaving early to seek safety. The grief eventually overcame my father; a nervous chain-smoker, he died from a heart attack at 61.

The Chain of Destiny

> The chain of destiny can only be grasped one link at a time.
> Winston Churchill

Unravelling the Past, 1990–2010

When I was growing up, I was warned not to speak to my father about his childhood or the war, as this would 'upset him'. I knew he had been born in Malaya and had been to boarding school but little else about his past. Later, I came across some envelopes in his stamp collection – sadly, they were empty but had contained letters his father had sent to him at school and gave their Malayan addresses – Sarasawatty Estate, Ipoh, Telok Anson, Bidor; exotic names of faraway places.

I was able to visit my father's childhood home on the rubber estate in Malaya just before he died. I brought back some Bidor chicken biscuits he remembered from his youth, which pleased him. Perhaps he would have been happy to talk about his early life after all.

The birth of my own children drove me to find out more about my family. I visited my father's elderly cousin in England – she had photos that were a wonderful insight into the family's life in the East. There were my grandparents in Melbourne on their wedding day – Anne standing in a thin dress that looks as though she has made it herself, and Colin seated, very young and tense, gripping the arms of a photo studio chair. Could they have had any idea of what their future would hold?

Another picture shows my grandfather's sister, Florence, known as Maie, as a young woman around 1900. Her rippling hair reaches nearly to the ground – such tresses could only have been managed by servants. Other photos show Maie at a Singapore garden party with her errant father,

Florence (Maie) Campbell, later Gordon, my grandfather's sister.

THE CHAIN OF DESTINY

John Campbell, the stationmaster, and her long-suffering mother. Several images show ladies in beaded 1920s dresses and men in tropical white suits at the Ipoh races. A further photo, the most revealing of all, shows Maie seated in a sedan chair being carried by bearers up the mountainside to the holiday resort at Maxwell Hill. The Campbells had truly enjoyed a rarefied life in Malaya.

The English cousin, Miss Sallie Goldie, had not known my father. Although born in Singapore in 1908, she had sailed to England in 1913 with her mother and brother to take him to boarding school. She retained a passenger list and menu from this German ship. The First World War broke out the following year, and Sallie and her mother had not been able to re-join her father working in Malaya. She told me many details of their life in the Far East, a taboo subject to me until then.

One story bears relating:

> Sallie's Mother Grace Goldie (the elder daughter of stationmaster John Campbell, and my grandfather's sister), believed in fortune tellers, hoping her life may hold a sudden change. The prediction was not good, however: 'I can see your husband in the arms of another woman,' the veiled mystic told her. Grace was in England, her husband working in Malaya – what could be done?
>
> Cabled news soon arrived that was even worse than imagined; her husband, Robert Murdoch Goldie, had died in Ipoh from complications of appendicitis. Grace's sister, Maie, had been at his bedside in the hospital, cradling him in her arms as he died.
>
> Robert had died on their wedding anniversary, which was also Sallie's birthday. A little later, a parcel arrived for Grace – Robert's anniversary gift of a Mizpah brooch, engraved 'Until We Meet Again'.

Maybe the lesson is that we should not ask to see the future – it may be vastly worse than we anticipate.

Malaya, 1920s.

The Lost Graves of Muntok

It was wonderful to meet Cousin Sallie in England, to hear her tales and her lovely tinkling laugh. But there was still a need to find out more about my father and grandfather.

My father's brother, Barney (Colin Bernard Campbell), had tried to find the location of their father's grave in Indonesia. He had written to the Australian Army and to the Commonwealth War Graves Commission. The CWGC replied that they were not responsible for the maintenance of civilian graves but had placed a book with the names of the Second World War civilian war dead in Westminster Abbey in London. The pages are turned to show names of different war casualties each day; the information can also be read on their website.

We saw in the CWGC online record that my grandfather, Colin Douglas Campbell, had died on 2 August 1944 in Muntok, Bangka Island, aged 53. The reporting authority was Sumatra, but the location of his grave is not given.

The CWGC wrote to my uncle again in August 1998, advising that his father's remains had been taken from Muntok in 1964 and reburied in an unmarked grave in a war cemetery in Bandung on the island of Java. A search of names in this cemetery reveals that only one named British civilian from the war is recorded as being buried in Bandung. This was not my grandfather.

The Grave Photograph

This situation of an unmarked grave was difficult to understand. My grandmother had a black and white photograph of my grandfather's grave in Muntok bearing his name and surrounded by many similar graves. The Muntok cemetery had been neatened after the war by the Dutch military, with a named wooden cross and a neat concrete surround made for each grave.

Internee William McDougall wrote that the civilian men had been buried by their friends in the Muntok town cemetery, also known as the old Dutch, civil or European cemetery, and that accurate details had been recorded of each grave location. The women's remains had been brought from graves within their prison camp into this Muntok cemetery just after the war.

We later learned that a detailed cemetery plan was made by the Dutch in 1948, showing rows and plot numbers. The Dutch military had taken a photograph of

THE LOST GRAVES OF MUNTOK

each grave in the Muntok cemetery after the war and placed advertisements in overseas newspapers offering the photos to bereaved relatives.

Where was my grandfather now?

We learned later that relatives of many of the prisoners had received these photos and, indeed, I have now seen them. The photos show an orderly and well-planned graveyard with each person's plot clearly marked and surrounded by graves of other internees, with recognisable names. It was hard to fathom how these graves had somehow become unmarked graves on a different Indonesian island.

The situation became more complex when the Netherlands War Graves Foundation (the Dutch sister organisation of the Commonwealth War Graves Commission), wrote to me that although they, the NWGF, had moved both the Dutch military and civilian graves from Muntok to Jakarta in 1964 and had contacted the British government at this time, advising them of this action, the British and Australian civilian graves had *not* been moved from Muntok.

This was very perplexing. Meanwhile, I explored any avenues that might lead to further information about the camps and the present location of this Muntok cemetery and the graves.

I read and reread *By Eastern Windows,* the book written by internee William McDougall, always finding new information. He describes how each coffin was suspended on ropes and poles, the poles then balanced on the shoulders of six prisoners. The bearers made their way through a park-like section of Muntok towards the cemetery. Because they were so weak, the men changed places with six others every quarter of a mile. McDougall wrote: 'The Old Dutch cemetery had been expanded for the internees and was expanding rapidly.'

DUTCH PICTURES OF WAR GRAVES
The Dutch War Graves Authorities have sent to Singapore photographs of the graves of civilian internees who were buried in Muntock Cemetery, Banka Island, Netherlands East Indies.

The photographs may be claimed by relatives, who should address their inquiries to Army Graves Registration, Nee Soon, Singapore.

Above left: The Straits Times, 9 November 1948, p.5.

Above right: Photograph of my grandfather's grave in Muntok, c.1948.

THE EVACUATION OF SINGAPORE

Disease-ridden PoW hospital.

McDougall tells how a simple service was held at the graveside with prayers spoken by Camp Leader Hal Hammett. As the coffin was placed in the ground, the Japanese guards saluted. Hammett next pushed a cross painted with the name of the deceased into the earth. The Japanese camp commandant provided wreaths for the graves, and the prisoners broke a few flowered stems from shrubs and laid them on the coffin.

Also very informative was the diary of internee Gordon Reis, who died in Muntok Jail. The diary is held at the Imperial War Museum in London and, at his family's request, is available to read online. This diary is a tragic record of Reis' 'slow death from starvation'. Reis' grave can be seen just behind and to the right of my grandfather's grave in the Muntok cemetery photo. We knew the Muntok cemetery had existed, but was it was still there?

Records of life and death in the women's camps were also invaluable. Australian nurses Betty Jeffrey's *White Coolies,* Pat Gunther's *Diary of a Nurse* and Jessie Simon's *While History Passed* (originally published under the title *In Japanese Hands*) and Researcher Lavinia Warner's *Women Beyond the Wire* all described the internees' lives and deaths in great detail.

The Past Comes to Life

A book review guided me to Desmond Woodford in Perth, Western Australia. Des had been a child in the camps. He first lived with his mother in the women's camp but was sent to live with the male prisoners as he reached puberty. Fortunately, his father was alive and among these men. Des discussed his life in the prison camps with American writer friend Susan McCabe, and she wrote a book, *Waiting for the Durian*, about Des' childhood. While weak and starving in Muntok Jail, young Des had sat and waited patiently for a large durian fruit in a tree overhanging the jail wall to ripen and fall. He knew if he was able to catch and eat it, the rich pulp might help him survive.

I telephoned and then visited Des and his wife Gillian. I learned that Des and his parents had escaped from Singapore on the *Giang Bee*, the same boat as my grandfather and Gordon Reis. Like them, Des' family had survived the bombing at sea and had reached Bangka Island. After the first weeks together in Muntok Jail, Des and his mother entered Irenelaan Women's Camp in Palembang. His father was placed first in Palembang Jail, then moved to the bamboo barracks camp, returned to Muntok and finally to Belalau. When Des and other boys showed signs of puberty, they were sent to Bangka Island to join the adult men in Muntok Jail. Distraught mothers and children did not know where the boys were going or if they would ever see one another again.

Des and Gillian informed me that Gillian's late older sister Edie (Betty) Leembruggen (nee Kenneison) and their grandparents had also been on board the *Giang Bee*. Her grandfather drowned when the ship was bombed, and Betty and her grandmother had been placed in the women's camps. During the years in camp, teenage Betty was helped and befriended by Australian Army Nurse Vivian Bullwinkel and the two had remained lifelong friends. Suddenly, I was able to hear details from someone who had been in both the men's and women's camps and whose wife had had a close relative there.

Next, a family newsletter found online quite by chance led me to contact and visit Neal Hobbs on Queensland's Sunshine Coast. Neal and his father had left Singapore on the *Mata Hari*, which travelled in convoy with the *Giang Bee* and the *Vyner Brooke*. Unlike most of the boats carrying evacuees that had been bombed and sunk, the *Mata Hari* had been captured and taken into Muntok Harbour. The passengers were then interned. Neal had been 17 years old in 1942 and had an adult's recollection of the harsh years that followed.

Neal's mother and his two sisters had left Singapore and reached Australia safely in early 1942, but Neal had chosen to stay in Malaya with his father. The two had gone to the shipping office in Singapore each day, amidst falling bombs, but had been refused exit permits until 12 February. They finally boarded the *Mata Hari* but did not reach safety – they were captured and interned for the next three and a half years.

Neal told me that when the *Mata Hari* was captured, the Japanese had poked bayonets at the chests of passengers. He had an empty tobacco tin in his breast pocket that was struck by a bayonet as he was threatened. He was spared injury but held the tin out to the soldier to show it was not a grenade.

Before she left Singapore, his mother had given Neal and her husband two diamond rings, which Neal hid between his toes in his sandshoes. Although it was uncomfortable for Neal to walk, the rings became a godsend in camp, to trade with local Indonesian people for food.

THE EVACUATION OF SINGAPORE

SS *Mata Hari*.

When the male internees were sent back to Muntok from Palembang in September 1943, a period when 270 men died from disease and starvation, 19-year-old Neal Hobbs had joined the burial party. Neal's father was a well-known horse trainer in Malaya. He had been a prize-winning jockey but had damaged his spine in a racing fall and was unable to work in camp. Neal took on the task of helping to bury his fellow internees – he received a little extra food for this task, which he gave to his father. They both survived.

Neal described how the dead were placed in rough wooden or bamboo coffins and carried by their friends to the town cemetery a mile (1.6km) away. Here, they were buried by men who had known them in normal working life before the war. The men sang the hymn 'Abide with Me' at the graveside before walking back to the jail. It was very likely that Neal had buried my grandfather.

> **Abide With Me (Henry Lyte)**
> Abide with me; fast falls the eventide;
> The darkness deepens; Lord, with me abide;
> When other helpers fail and comforts flee,
> Help of the helpless, oh abide with me.
> Swift to its close ebbs out life's little day;
> Earth's joys grow dim, its glories pass away;
> Change and decay in all around I see –
> O Thou who changes not, abide with me.
> I fear no foe, with Thee at hand to bless;
> Ills have no weight, and tears no bitterness;
> Where is death's sting? Where, grave, thy victory?
> I triumph still, if Thou abide with me.

All comforts *had* fled, the internees were 'the helpless' and decay was all around. But I wonder if there was a certain defiance as the prisoners sang the words 'I fear no foe' and 'I triumph still' in the presence of the Japanese guards?

THE LOST GRAVES OF MUNTOK

Bamboo coffin.

Ubi Kayu, Under the Wire, Belalau Men's Camp, 1 March 1945 to October 1945

Neal Hobbs had been born in Malaya and had left Singapore as it struggled and fell. He told me of work at the Muntok aerodrome, where men feared they would be killed, hardships of daily life in the men's camps in Palembang, Muntok and Belalau, anecdotes about fellow prisoners and the many funerals.

It is so important to hear these past events at first hand. Internee William McDougall's camp diaries and book, *By Eastern Windows*, document life in the men's camps in great detail, but Neal had experienced the camps and had known and remembered the inhabitants. He had a wonderful and detailed memory and was happy to answer my many questions.

Neal turned 21 in Belalau camp, and all the men in his hut signed his birthday card, which is still a treasured family possession. The names read like a roll call of Australian internees – Mr Wootton, Australian government staff member in Singapore under executed official Mr Vivian Bowden; Donnelly the jockey; Leslie McCann, who crept out from camp with Neal foraging for food; and Amby Marning, my grandparents' friend and neighbour in Malaya.

Neal told how he and McCann had 'gone under the wire' several times at Belalau, crawling beneath the barbed wire fence to look for food. Their goal was to find ubi roots growing in the wild or in farmers' fields. The ubi could be boiled or fried in lamp oil and eaten or sold to internees who still had money. This hunting could only be done on the darkest nights. Even so, tigers, snakes and other wild animals in the surrounding jungle were always a hazard, as was the risk of being caught on returning to camp.

On one dreadful occasion, Neal was seen by a guard while coming back to camp at dawn with his sack of ubi roots. Neal dropped the bag before he was accosted and denied he had been outside the wire. He was placed in a hut, where he was threatened and beaten throughout the day but refused to confess, knowing the consequence may be death.

THE EVACUATION OF SINGAPORE

Hal Hammett, the elected British camp leader, pleaded with the Japanese commandant for many hours to free him. In Neal's favour was the fact that, like his jockey father, he was short. He was then 20 years old but, being very undernourished, feels the Japanese probably took him for a child and finally let him go. Neal did not leave the camp to look for ubi kayu roots again.

Neal and Hal Hammett, who had helped to save his life, both returned to work in Malaya after the war. They played bridge together but never discussed their internment or this episode.

The *Li Wo*

Neal's foraging partner, Richard Leslie McCann, was a gold miner from Malaya. He had left Singapore on a small Yangtze River steamer, the *Li Wo*, which became surrounded by Japanese warships in the Bangka Strait off Muntok. There being no hope of escape, Captain Thomas Wilkinson gave the order to fire.

The *Li Wo*, with only one small gun manned by McCann, gave fire, sinking one Japanese ship and damaging another, before she was blown apart. There were only eight survivors, one of whom was Leslie McCann. Like Vivian Bullwinkel, McCann concealed his experiences while in camp in case of reprisals. After the war, Captain Wilkinson was awarded a posthumous Victoria Cross.

Leslie McCann survived the war but died at an early age from heart disease, most likely a consequence of beriberi and malnutrition.

Above: The *Li Wo*.

Left: Captain Wilkinson.

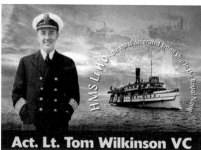

THE LOST GRAVES OF MUNTOK

Australia 2010, Donald Frederick Pratt

In 2010, a most unexpected event occurred. Cousin Sallie's mother's fortune teller could not have predicted anything more surprising, nor any of the events that followed…

Some years earlier, I had joined BACSA, the British Association for Cemeteries in South Asia, seeking information about my great-grandfather, John Colin Campbell, the Geraldton, Fremantle and Malayan stationmaster. He had died in Singapore in 1902 and was buried there in the Bukit Timah cemetery. The area had been destroyed in a battle against the Japanese in February 1942. The grave was overtaken by jungle, and I learned that the cemetery records had been eaten by white ants.

BACSA required overseas members to join for life. I did this and thus received the three-monthly magazines thereafter. Most editions related to Colonial India, but one memorable day in 2010, an article leapt up before my eyes. I opened the new booklet of BACSA'S journal *Chowkidar* to read that Anthony Pratt in London was seeking the grave of his father, Donald Frederick Pratt, a civilian who had died in 1945 in Muntok. Mr Pratt's solicitor friend was investigating for him and had been told by the Commonwealth War Graves' Commission that Donald Pratt's grave had been moved from Muntok on Bangka Island to Bandung in Java.

I wrote to Mr Pratt through BACSA explaining I believed that our relatives' graves had *not* been moved and were still in Muntok. Days later, Mr Pratt flew to Australia to meet former internees Neal Hobbs and Ralph Armstrong in Brisbane and Des Woodford in Perth to ask if they remembered his father. I accompanied Anthony to meet them.

Amazingly, all three men did recall Anthony Pratt's father. Donald Pratt had been active in the prison camp concerts in Palembang and was remembered as the nephew of Hollywood film horror actor Boris Karloff. He had also worked as a camp barber cutting internees' hair for a few cents. He had developed renal failure following his forced labouring at Pladjoe and had died in Muntok on Easter Sunday 1945, remaining in the care of Dr Lentze as he was too ill to travel to the final camp at Belalau. He was 34 years old.

Where are They Now?

> Grief knits hearts in closer bonds than happiness ever can;
> Common sufferings are far stronger links than common joys
> Alphonse de Lamartine, 1790–1869

The Muntok Civilian Graves

In Brisbane, Ralph Armstrong told us that he and his nephew in England, both former child internees, had tried for many years to find what had become of the civilian Muntok Prison Camp graves. Ralph's mother and his sister Dixie had died in Muntok; his sister Grace, his nephew's mother, had died at Belalau. He showed us a summary of correspondence between a former internee, Mrs Shelagh Lea (nee Brown), and the British Government; letters now held in the British National Archives in Kew.

Mrs Lea had lost her mother and numerous friends in camp. She had written to the British Government for decades after the war, asking for the Muntok graves to be preserved or at least for a memorial to be placed in the town.

At first, the replies Mrs Lea received from the British Foreign Office were favourable – they wrote that the Dutch authorities planned to make concrete edges around each Muntok grave and to plant flowering verbenas on the plots. The Commonwealth War Graves Commission advised Mrs Lea that they had no responsibility for civilian graves. Later, British authorities wrote to her to suggest that local churches in Indonesia could raise funds to take care of these British and Australian civilian graves. They even recommended that Mrs Lea should raise money herself for the upkeep of the Muntok cemetery or the construction of a memorial. Shelagh Lea was married to an Anglican minister in a remote area of Canada and had no funds for this type of undertaking.

Other correspondence from the British Government regarding Second World War civilian graves, also held in the National Archives in Kew, expressed concerns that if the graves of European internees were cared for, this would be a precedent for the many graves of 'Asiatic Natives', who had died as prisoners of the Japanese on the Thai Burma railway, to also be maintained.

An Indonesian religious minister had visited Muntok for his holidays in 1968 and taken photographs in the town (known as the old Dutch or civil) cemetery.

WHERE ARE THEY NOW?

His photographs show a large number of British and Australian graves still standing with intact crosses. The minister had also compiled lists of names visible on both upright and leaning crosses, confirming that many graves were still in place and were fully identifiable at that time. This was well after the Dutch graves had been moved to Jakarta in the early 1960s and confirmed that our families' graves had indeed been left behind.

In 1981, the Netherlands War Graves Foundation had visited Muntok on behalf of Anthony Pratt. Their thorough investigation also concluded that the vast majority of British and Australian civilian graves had *not* been moved to Jakarta. The Netherlands War Graves Foundation wrote to me that the Muntok cemetery had been built over by a petrol station in 1981 and that houses now also stood on the site.

Above and right: Abandoned British and Australian graves, Muntok. Photos taken by a visiting religious minister from Palembang in 1968.

THE EVACUATION OF SINGAPORE

O.M. Bekker's grave, courtesy Muntok Heritage Community.

I contacted a petroleum engineer from Bangka Island asking for information about the location of the petrol station now overlying the graves. He forwarded my query to Muhammed Rizki, the manager of Timah Tin in Muntok. Mr Rizki very kindly emailed photos of the modern Pertamina petrol station and surrounding houses in Muntok now on the cemetery site.

Mr Rizki also sent a photo of a grave, that of O.M.W. Bekker, in the old Muntok Cemetery. The cemetery is identical to the photos we held of our families' graves and the graves of internees Gordon Burt and R.J.Strong can be clearly seen.

I knew we had found the right place.

A local family in Muntok looked for our relatives' graves for us in the area around the Pertamina petrol station but were unable to find them. A modern cemetery adjoins the area, but the former internees' graves were not visible.

Our Journey

An invisible thread connects those who are destined to meet.

Chinese Proverb

April 2011, Palembang, South Sumatra, Indonesia

In April 2011, Anthony Pratt and I decided to travel to Muntok to see where our families had been imprisoned and if any light could be thrown on the matter of the missing graves.

We met in Singapore, then flew to Palembang to try to find where the internees had been imprisoned there. As our plane circled Palembang to land, we saw fields and small houses, palm trees and the wide curling Moesi River below. It was easy to imagine the town as it had been nearly seventy years ago.

We were very lucky to meet a guide in Palembang, Pak Abisofyan, from the Sultan Mahmud Badaruddin Museum, near the Kuto Besak fort on the Moesi (or 'Mosquito') River. The museum is an imposing building with a sweeping double staircase outside – we learned it had been taken over as Japanese headquarters during the war. Our guide walked with us to the Independence Memorial, with a graphic mural showing the harshness of life under Japanese rule.

From here, we crossed the busy road to Palembang Jail. The men imprisoned there had said this period was less difficult than the later camps. They were healthier and had hopes of release. Food was limited, though, and dysentery and deficiency diseases began. Sir John Campbell, 2nd Baronet, who was awarded the Croix de Guerre in the First World War, had trapped sparrows with a noose on the ground of the jail exercise yard to eat them.

Medical supplies were limited in Palembang Jail, but staff improvised with very few

Detail from the Independence Memorial, Palembang.

THE EVACUATION OF SINGAPORE

Palembang Jail, where the men spent their first year.

resources. Doctors West, Hollweg and Boema and volunteers bathed internees' leg ulcers and treated the painful rashes of 'Palembang Bottom'. This was helped firstly by sitting in a bucket of hot water. Next, blisters on the tender buttock and scrotal skin were punctured and painted with gentian violet, followed by naked sunbathing, with good results.

The *Camp News* magazine advertised for old clothes to be torn up for dysentery rags to bathe the patients. The foul rags were washed daily, dried in the sun and used again. Some patients were able to be treated at the Catholic Charitas Hospital and taken there in trucks. Here they were cared for by Dutch doctors and nursing nuns and the German internee Dr Annamaria Goldberg, until the hospital was forcibly closed by the Japanese in September 1943. At this time, doctors had been beheaded or imprisoned and the Bishop of Palembang, Muntok priest, Catholic brothers and nuns sent to the prison camps.

The internees in Palembang Jail distracted themselves with language classes and lectures. Gordon Burt spoke of his experiences as chief engineer in the British Arctic Expedition to the North Pole in 1925, where he met with a polar bear, and planter H.P. Kendall spoke on 'How I shot a tiger with a revolver'. Both these brave men later died in camp. Gordon Burt had received an OBE in January 1942 for his work with the Armoured Car (Tank) Division of the Singapore Volunteer Forces. He had learned Spanish and the ukulele in camp to surprise his wife when he returned home. Sadly, this was not to be. He died in Muntok in January 1945 from beriberi and starvation, becoming one of the many Muntok lost graves.

The typed, hand-coloured issues of *Camp News,* two in English and two in Dutch, were read avidly and were passed on to the next reader. The men organised well-attended several concerts, held on the nights of a tropical full moon. A badminton tournament took place, and, on another occasion, men laid bets on a human piggy-back horse race to raise funds for the women's camp Christmas meal.

Life was not easy, however, and constant worry and uncertainty over health, family, friends and the future occupied many long, dreary hours. Some could not bear the strain – one man escaped, only to be shot dead in the Moesi River, and several tried to take their lives.

In April 1943, after the men had moved from Palembang Jail to the new atap and bamboo camp, the Japanese Kempeitai or secret police seized English nurses Margot Turner, Olga Neubronner, Jenny MacAlister and Mary Cooper and Dr Hollweg's wife. These women were placed in solitary confinement in Palembang Jail for six months for no known reason. The local prisoners in the jail – murderers and thieves – tried to help the women, sometimes passing a banana, black coffee or a piece of cake to them through the cell bars. Olga wrote long poems on her cell wall. One described packing her wedding dress to leave Singapore, and all sent loving messages to her soldier husband. Olga had delivered a stillborn son on Muntok pier in February 1942. She and Mary were much weakened by imprisonment in the jail and both later died in camp.

Palembang Jail, a high-walled, foreboding building topped with coils of barbed wire, is still in use as a prison, now for women. Conditions are vastly improved, with good food, a daily menu, medical and pastoral care and vocational training. Prisoners run a commercial kitchen in the jail, with produce sold in a bakery just outside. Women learn skills such as sewing, hairdressing and mushroom farming to help them find work on their release.

Our guide helped us to find a bookshop and buy a large-scale map of modern Palembang. We were able to compare this map with Dutch Second World War maps from the East Indies Camp Archives website. The old Dutch maps clearly indicate the men's and women's camps. Two distinctively shaped lakes could be seen on both the old and new maps, and roads had also maintained their outline. Suddenly, the locations of the Dutch Houses Camp (Irenelaan) at Bukit Besar and the nearby barracks camp built by the men became clear!

Our helpful guide took us on a local bus to the district of Talang Semoet, and we walked through the suburbs. We recognised landscapes described by William McDougall in *By Eastern Windows*, in the camp diaries of Gordon Reis and Gordon Burt and from books written after the war by Dutch internee Helen Colijn, Australian nurses Betty Jeffrey and Jessie Symons and by film producer Lavinia Warner.

The compact Dutch houses that formed the women's camp of Irenelaan remain in Jalan Dr Cipto and Jalan Teuku Umar, although the bamboo and atap huts built by the men and later used by the women are long gone, replaced by large, modern homes near Jalan Sumatera. We wondered if current residents know what happened here so long ago – the suffering, the human effort and struggle to survive?

THE EVACUATION OF SINGAPORE

House lived in by Australian Army nurses, Jalan Dr Cipto.

Talang Semoet, Palembang (Former Irenelaan Camp)

We followed the likely route taken by the men as they had walked from Palembang Jail to build their prison huts from bamboo and palm leaves. A long, mildewed brick wall stood near the houses that had formed the Irenelaan Women's Camp.

Wall, former Irenelaan Women's Camp, Jalan Cipto, Palembang.

We wondered if this was where the women had stood, waving and singing to the men each day as they walked past to build the new camp.

We recalled internee William McDougall's moving description of Christmas Eve and Boxing Day 1942. Then, the women had stood on the wall, waiting quietly. As the men approached, the women had begun singing Christmas carols to them across the field. Gordon Burt was part of the men's working party that day. In the distance, he saw a nun's arms waving, conducting the women's choir, and heard the strains of their voices. The men reciprocated with songs as they walked to work on Boxing Day. The groups could not speak together but at least saw and heard loved ones and friends in the distance and knew that they were still alive.

This knowledge and hearing the well-known music was more precious than any gift. As McDougall wrote, this Christmas, although difficult and after a terrible year, was more meaningful for many than ever experienced before.

Anton Colijn managed to crawl through the long grass and see his three daughters at the women's camp, passing them a cooked chicken. He later died in camp, and the girls did not see their father again.

Charitas Hospital, Palembang, 2011 (Rumah Sakit Charitas)

I had written to Charitas Hospital in Palembang and we were invited to visit. We were warmly welcomed by the director, Professor Hardi Darmawan and the nursing nuns. Charitas is now a large, modern multi-storey hospital, although a small area of old buildings remain. It is a short drive from the site of the former internment camps. Some men, women and children from the civilian camps and captive soldiers from the military camps in Palembang were taken in trucks for treatment before the hospital was forcibly closed. A small cemetery lay behind the hospital for those who died in the wards, but no prisoners' graves are visible now.

Until the hospital was closed by the Japanese in 1943, the Charitas doctors and nurses had done everything possible to help the internees and the prisoners of war held in the Palembang military prison camps at the Mulo and Cheung Wa Schools, Sungei Geron and the airport. As well as providing medical care under great difficulty, staff had helped patients to smuggle medicine, money and messages back into the camps.

In September 1943, Australian Army Nurse Mavis Hannah was found carrying letters back into the women's camp, hidden in a sanitary napkin. Other such episodes were detected. Staff were accused of spying, and the Japanese Army closed the hospital with tragic consequences. Doctors were imprisoned or beheaded. Reverend Mother Alocoque was sent to a severe military prison, where she knelt and prayed while she was tortured. She was one of a few prisoners to survive this prison. Forty nuns were interned in Palembang Women's Camp.

On leaving Charitas for camp, the nuns concealed medicines, instruments and bandages under their habits.

A bronze plaque hangs in Charitas Hospital's foyer, given in memory of the Allied soldiers, sailors and airmen from the military camps who were treated at Charitas during the war. This is a fine tribute to the hospital for the help provided during the harsh war years in such difficult circumstances. The Charitas nuns were given a Distinguished Service Medal by Britain's King George after the war, and this is treasured in the nun's museum.

Pladjoe, 2011

In the evening, our guide Abisofyan escorted us downstream on the Moesi River in a small wooden motor boat to see the oil refineries of Pladjoe. We travelled through the twilight along the expanse of olive-green water, past wooden stilt houses standing in the water and aqua- and orange-painted fishing boats. It was Friday, and the call to prayer from many minarets rang out clearly.

Anthony's father and many others had been forced to labour at Pladjoe for the Japanese. As we travelled, we thought of Donald Pratt, Gordon Reis and all who had been made to work in these oil fields. Donald Pratt's health had broken down irreparably, while others had died here from dysentery. Their friends had burnt their bodies in this camp.

In February 1942, the Japanese had fought for control of the oil-rich fields of Sumatra. A Japanese air fleet flew in droves and carried paratroopers to land and fight in the Battle of Palembang. These Japanese planes had flown over the Bangka Strait just as evacuees from Singapore were sailing below and, together with warships travelling to Palembang, had bombed them relentlessly.

Our guide told us about his uncle, an Indonesian boy of 16 in 1942. The lad was forced to help the Japanese under threat of harm to his family. He was given a rifle and made to stand in the refinery complex at Pladjoe, next to the huge oil tanks. He was ordered to point his gun upwards and shoot at any Dutch or British planes overhead. It is a terrible image – a young boy next to a volatile oil tank that would have exploded in a firestorm if hit from above.

Pladjoe, Moesi River, Palembang.

The End of the Road

> When we did reach the shore, we found ourselves among mangroves. They were too thick to struggle through and as the tide was going out and threatening to sweep us out to sea again, we decided to climb into the tree tops for the night.
>
> We tried not to think about crocodiles. And when we did see 'logs' in the water below us, we told ourselves they were just logs.
>
> Nursing Sister Iole Harper, *The West Australian*, Tuesday, 25 September 1945, p.6

The town of Muntok is the most western tip of Bangka Island and is known as 'the end of the road'. It was just this for many.

Muntok, 2011, Bangka Island

Early next morning, we began our journey to Muntok. We drove through the quiet darkness of Palembang to arrive at the Boom Baru docks on the Moesi River. We waited as the ferry was loaded; the bustle of people and packages a contrast to the vast, quiet water. This river, which had transported the internees back and forth from Bangka Island in increasing states of distress, ill-health and in ever-diminishing numbers, was calm and beautiful in the early morning.

Dawn broke suddenly, as happens in the Far East. We watched the sky turn from navy to orange, then pink and misty pearl over the water.

Our transport from Palembang to Muntok was the Express Bahari jetfoil. The journey, which had taken the prisoners a full day or more, took us three hours. For the first two hours, we travelled slowly along the wide brown river, past Pladjoe oil refinery, floating wooden homes and colourful fishing boats. The scene then became one of mangrove swamps and tangles of dense jungle creepers. Last came an hour's ride across the ocean of the Bangka Strait. The trip in the carpeted VIP cabin was comfortable, with air-conditioning, a washroom, refreshments and a TV playing Indonesian movies and songs. It was vastly different from the journeys endured by the internees, confined in foul barges for over twenty-six hours, cramped, stifling and with no comforts or facilities at all.

THE EVACUATION OF SINGAPORE

Early morning sky, Moesi River.

As we approached Muntok, we ventured outside the cabin. The air was fresh and clean, the sea a clear turquoise. The red and white lighthouse came into view, growing larger. We had finally arrived, to seek more information about where our relatives had been buried in 1944 and 1945 and to learn what had become of their graves after the war.

We had been apprehensive about visiting Muntok, where our families had experienced such hardship and tragedy, but after our visit were left with positive impressions and had made many new friends. We spent three days on Bangka Island and found exceptional kindness and interest in our quest.

We were met at Muntok Harbour by Mr Fakhrizal Abubakar, a representative of the Timah Tin Company and the Muntok Heritage Community. He drove us into the small town, past bright wooden houses and lush tropical growth, palm trees, creepers and purple bougainvilleas. Mr Rizki, the manager of Timah Tin, and members of the Muntok Heritage Community welcomed us. We enjoyed a picnic lunch together and watched a community mangrove planting at the edge of the sea. It was good to see this action to protect the environment.

The Former Muntok Town, Civil or Old Dutch Cemetery

After lunch, our hosts took us to the Pertamina petrol station situated on the main road through Muntok, one mile from the jail. This was the location of the cemetery as described in internee William McDougall's books and in Shelagh Lea's post-war letters to the British Government, where she had requested preservation of the internees' graves.

The petrol station is next to a small modern cemetery, but there is evidence of very old graves nearby. Residents from houses behind the petrol station showed us some worn grave stones lying in their gardens – one was for Isabella Inkster, who had died at sea in 1881. There was no sign of any internees' graves; however, we learned some vital facts.

One of the residents told us he had played in the former cemetery behind the petrol station when he was a child in the 1960s. This area is now built over with several houses. It is accessed through a paved stone gateway flanked by stone pillars and along a dirt path, Gang Durian 'Durian Lane', called after the delicious but odorous fruit. The man showed us where the boundary walls of the cemetery had been. He agreed that the graves at that time had appeared just as in our photographs, with neat concrete surrounds and wooden crosses bearing the names of the deceased.

Members of the Heritage Community showed us the photograph of Dutch Internee O.M.W. Bekker's grave, which Mr Rizki had sent us earlier. The photo had been taken by local resident and photographer Mr Syarifudin in the 1960s at the site where we now stood. Mr Syarifudin was President Sukarno's English interpreter during his exile in Muntok. His son, who accompanied us to the cemetery, was a member of the Heritage Community. This photograph matched our own photos in every way, with the same style of graves and crosses. Names were clearly visible on the crosses in the picture; internee Gordon Burt's grave is clearly seen to the left of Mr Bekker's and that of R.J. Strong to the right. This was definitely the place we were seeking.

The man who had played in the cemetery then described seeing graves exhumed in the early 1960s, with bodies placed in bags with individual metal name plates. This was inconsistent with the Commonwealth War Graves Commission's statement that civilians who died in Muntok had been reburied in Java in one unmarked grave. We recalled the words of the CWGC, which maintain they 'have no responsibility for civilian graves' and who today state that their charter cannot be changed to provide graves or memorials for civilians.

The Netherlands War Graves Foundation informed us they had moved all Dutch military and civilian graves from Muntok to war cemeteries in Java in 1964. The British had been contacted but had not accepted the Dutch offer to move their civilian graves. A small number of British and Australian graves were moved by the Dutch. These included people who wore a uniform in daily life, such as members of the police or St John's Ambulance and some Malayan and Singapore Volunteers, perhaps mistaken for enlisted military personnel. The graves of crew from the Empress of Asia and the Singapore Broadcasting Commission were later moved to Java by their employers. But for most prisoners who died in Muntok, there is no record of their ever having been moved.

The Indonesian church minister holidaying from Palembang in 1968 had taken photos and made lists of names from the many intact and identifiable graves in the

THE EVACUATION OF SINGAPORE

Pertamina petrol station, Muntok.

Muntok town cemetery. We were now sure that our families had not been exhumed in 1964 and that they still lie in this place.

Householders living behind the petrol station showed an interest in our exploration and came to speak to us. They told how they had uncovered human remains, bones, hair and teeth as they dug the foundations for their homes in the late 1960s. This did not seem to bother the residents. They also told stories of a ghost who frequents their homes – a tall, headless man in a military uniform, who they said does not trouble them.

We hastened to explain to householders that we definitely did not want to pull down their homes to exhume our relatives but just wanted to know where they had been buried and where they very likely still lie. A house will soon be built on vacant land behind the petrol station, and it will be interesting to learn if any further remains are found there. We asked if we could please be informed of any findings.

The Catholic Cemetery, Kampong Menjelang, Muntok

We had now gained the trust of our new friends, who drove us to a large Catholic cemetery. They explained that this was near Kampong Menjelang, the former site of the women's prison camp. Further news awaited us here.

Graves with remains of twenty-five people moved from Pertamina petrol station to Muntok Catholic cemetery, 1981 (refurbished in 2015 as a memorial grave, with names of all prisoners remaining in Muntok).

In this large Catholic cemetery, with many recent headstones, were three older graves standing together at the front, near the roadside. The two graves on either side were flat, while the central grave had a concrete engraved headstone. Mr Rizki translated the inscription to read:

> Here lie 25 English people, victims of the Japanese War, who died between 1942 and 1945, buried here in March 1981.

We were told that these twenty-five bodies had been found and recovered during the building of the Pertamina petrol station in 1981 and given by the petrol station owner to the Catholic priest for reburial. This added further weight to our conviction that Muntok town cemetery had not been fully emptied and that the remains of our families had *not* been moved to Java in 1964.

Penjara – Muntok Jail

We were very privileged to visit Muntok Jail, the former men's camp, which is still in use as a men's prison. We filed in through the heavy gates and felt we had stepped back in time. The prisoners are well cared for today with adequate food and recreation, but we recognised William McDougall's description of the high walls, barred cells and dormitories with concrete slabs for sleeping. A grove of tall durian trees stands outside the rear wall of the jail; these had once provided the child Des Woodford with a lifesaving piece of fruit, for which he sat on the ground patiently waiting for it to fall.

The jail has the capacity for 250 men – it was hard to picture that nearly 1,000 prisoners were once crowded inside. It was from Muntok Jail and the adjoining coolie lines (now demolished) that the burial party would carry the dead men to the town cemetery. In the second half of 1944 and in early 1945, between four and six men died from disease and starvation daily. When there were several deaths in a day, the Japanese provided a hand cart for the internees to pull their dead friends the long, hard mile through the heat to the graveyard. The prisoners had starved through lack of food, but the prison camp commandant had donated elaborate floral wreaths for funerals.

Kampong Menjelang, the Muntok Women's Camp

Our friends from the Heritage Community then took us to the site of the former women's camp, close to the Catholic cemetery. Many families now live here in Kampong Menjelang village next to a large playing field. Today, only a stone well remains to tell of the hundreds of women and child prisoners who lived and worked here and the many who died in their bamboo and palm leaf prison.

We were introduced to an older lady who showed us a gold and diamond ring – a fine gold band with a single small stone. She told us this was given to her father-in-law by a lady prisoner in return for food for her children. The family has kept this ring carefully in a small box for the past seventy years. She also has a fob watch, Robinsons' brand, engraved with number 2029877, given in exchange for food. In Muntok, this lady is known as 'the Mother with the Ring'.

Robinsons is a Singapore department store but does not have older records detailing watch sales. We have also contacted watch-sellers D.M. Robinson in the UK but as yet have not been able to find the name of the owner of this watch.

THE EVACUATION OF SINGAPORE

Above left: Original well from women's prison camp, still in use by Muntok residents.

Above right: Former internee Neal Hobbs, Judy Balcombe and 'the Mother with the Ring'.

We met other older residents who had been in Muntok during the war. Everywhere, we found people eager to talk and to tell us their experiences. We were made welcome and offered kindness, refreshments and information at every home.

Japanese planes had bombed Muntok in early February 1942, killing local residents and destroying homes. They had then landed from warships in great numbers. Local women were attacked by Japanese soldiers. One Dutch-Indonesian lady told us she had dyed her hair black as a teenager to avoid being assaulted. Some girls had cut their hair and dressed as boys. An older man remembered hearing and seeing the Japanese planes overhead.

We visited the house of Mr Afan, who lived in Muntok as a child. In 1942, he was aged 9. Mr Afan recalled seeing children in the women's camp looking out hungrily through the wire. He wished to help them but was afraid of the Japanese guards.

Mr Afan spoke to us slowly and clearly in English, retrieving his memories:

> In February (10th February) 1942, bombs from Japanese planes fell on Muntok. One fell on our house, which was burnt down. On 16th February, many Japanese soldiers landed in Muntok; they came ashore in four transport vessels. We rented a house for a few days until on Friday, 20th February, my parents and many other people decided to hide in the country.
>
> Two policemen told us to be ready to leave at exactly 8pm. We walked quietly through the bushes, carrying our possessions. Many villagers sheltered under a great rock named Batu Balai, the Meeting Place, for forty days and nights.

Batu Balai, the great rock and meeting place.

THE END OF THE ROAD

Eventually a proclamation came from the Japanese commandant, ordering us to return home and to work again.

In Muntok, some Japanese soldiers were billeted opposite our house. Some young men used to come and speak to my mother – perhaps they missed their own mothers in Japan.

Food was scarce for the residents of Muntok. Soon there was no rice and we had to dig for ubi (tapioca) roots. One day my mother and I were gathering wild fruit near the women's (internment) camp. The children in the camp, behind the barbed wire, were thin and hungry and held out their hands begging for some fruit. I wanted to give them some of our fruit, but we were too afraid of the Japanese guards with their rifles and sharp bayonets.

This happened seventy years ago but I still feel sad and wish I could have given some fruit to these children.

We visited Mrs Abdurrachim, who owns the large house opposite the Tinwinning Building and the Muntok Jail. It is her home and is also a homestay for visitors. During the war, this house was used by Japanese camp commandant Captain Seiki Kazue as his residence and office. It was an unusual feeling to walk slowly through the large rooms, with high ceilings and traditional Dutch architecture, knowing that Captain Seiki had taken over the building and had lived and worked here. Mrs Abdurrachim asked me to accept a crocheted tissue box cover she had made. It was very warming to feel her friendship and to know that the Sudirman Homestay is now a happy family home.

Above left and above right: Sudirman Homestay, house used by Captain Seiki Kazue.

Radji Beach and Nurses' Memorial

Our hosts in Muntok were kindness personified and continued to show us important historical sites. One afternoon, they took us by motorboat through the ocean for

THE EVACUATION OF SINGAPORE

twenty minutes to the site of the massacre of the Australian Army nurses, civilians and servicemen, at the place now known as Radji Beach.

The beach is accessible either by boat, along a long, rough road or by a four-hour walk through the jungle. The area is also known as 'English Bay' after the European people who were killed there on 16 February 1942. It was hard to imagine that this peaceful and lovely bay, with turquoise water and pure white sand, had been the site of such atrocities.

We walked on the quiet shore trying to identify the two streams where the shipwrecked victims found water and the headland where the men were taken to be killed. We chose some small pebbles as treasures to take home. They were rich in iron and deep red but to us looked stained with blood.

Skeletons of sunken boats litter the shore, whether brought to stop erosion or from actual ships bombed after leaving Singapore, no one is sure, but they serve as a poignant reminder of the tragedy of February 1942.

We met a man whose family had helped either the wounded Vivian Bullwinkel and Private Cecil Kinsley or servicemen who escaped from Muntok before the groups were first moved to Palembang. After the war, the Australian Government gave this man's father an A£50 reward. He gave us a copy of the much-revered document. It was, however, little compensation to the villagers who had fled their homes in fear of Japanese reprisal and had never returned.

A memorial to the nurses stands near the Muntok lighthouse at Tanjong Kelian, overlooking the Bangka Strait. This site is not at Radji Beach, which is isolated

Above left: Nurses' memorial, Tanjong Kelian, Muntok.

Above right: Muntok lighthouse, Tanjong Kelian.

Left: Wrecked boats off Muntok.

THE END OF THE ROAD

and several kilometres from Muntok, but was later chosen by Vivian Bullwinkel as a more accessible place. Two winking lighthouses had been beacons guiding the shipwrecked victims to shore. A portion of stone from the women's camp kitchen and latrines was used to form the base of the memorial.

Vivian Bullwinkel and other surviving nurses and family members gathered with Indonesian and Australian authorities in 1993 to dedicate the memorial. By chance, Anthony Pratt and I visited the Memorial on Anzac Day, 25th April, which remembers all Australians and New Zealanders who serve or die in war. There was no ceremony or bugles or prayers that morning, no official recognition, only two people whose families had been so damaged by this War. We left some artificial poppies in memory of all who suffered here.

Plans for a Museum

We learned that the Muntok Heritage Community planned to create a museum in the Tinwinning Building, opposite the jail that had served as the men's prison camp. This museum would cover the history of Bangka Island, its tin mining industry and would also have a section relating to the war years. We asked the Heritage Community if it would please be possible to place a plaque to remember the internees, including those who died in Muntok and have no marked grave.

The imposing Tinwinning Building had been the head office of the Timah Tin mining company. During the war, sick and dying men were placed in the so-called 'hospital' in the coolie lines (now demolished) to the right of Muntok Jail. Here, my grandfather and Anthony Pratt's father and many other male prisoners died. The dedicated interned doctors, Catholic brothers and the men's friends tried to help the patients suffering from malaria, dysentery, beriberi, TB and starvation. There was no medicine and few resources, but the men were lovingly cared for and never died alone.

After trying for so long to have the internees remembered, it was heartening for us to know that their lives and stories would not be forgotten, through the commitment, enthusiasm and kindness of our new Indonesian friends.

Timah Tinwinning Museum, Jalan Sudirman, Muntok.

Remember Me

When you dream, remember me
I am the quiet beneath a churning sea
I am the froth on a burning wave
The silver light that shines upon
The stillness of forever and beyond
                        Eira Day, daughter of child internee Harry Dyne

Memorial Plaques, February 2012

Anthony Pratt and I were very moved after our first visit to Palembang and Muntok. We had been made so welcome and had learned a great deal. In particular, we were reminded that the Muntok internees had no named graves or memorial.

On seeing the plaque in the foyer of Charitas Hospital that thanked staff for their lifesaving care of military prisoners of war in 1942 and 1943, we decided to investigate placing plaques in memory of the internees. The responses from Professor Hardi Darmawan at Charitas and from our friends in Muntok were favourable, so we proceeded, seeking a manufacturing company and choosing suitable words. In Melbourne, I contacted A1 Plaques, which had been well recommended. This company had made plaques for war graves at Gallipoli and in New Guinea and for many local organisations.

The Malayan Volunteers Group (MVG) very kindly offered to fund plaques for Palembang and Muntok. The MVG is formed of families and friends of people who had lived in pre-war Malaya and Singapore and who had served in the Volunteer Forces there. Historians and other interested people are also welcome to join. A number of MVG members, including Neal Hobbs, Vilma Howe, Jane Elgey and the late Ralph Armstrong and Des Woodford, were interned as children. The aim of MVG is to increase knowledge and understanding of this period and to bring together families with similar experiences.

Before the war, it was compulsory for men under 50 years of age to join the Volunteer Forces, to defend the Malay Peninsula, as non-commissioned soldiers. They were compelled to keep their regular jobs, training after hours and attending camps. They underwent serious drill training in uniform, learning to handle weapons. There were also armoured car (tank) divisions.

REMEMBER ME

As the Japanese advanced towards Singapore, the Volunteers were not permitted to leave. This led to thousands of European and Eurasian civilians remaining in Singapore until they were finally allowed to evacuate. Permits allowing people to board boats were belatedly issued in mid-February 1942, just days before the fall. The many boats carrying evacuees had then been attacked by Japanese planes and warships, where huge numbers were killed or had drowned.

Survivors from these boats were interned by the Japanese in prison camps, where men, women and children slowly perished. Although the Volunteers had trained and many fought in Malaya and Singapore alongside commissioned soldiers, those who survived the war or families of the deceased were not entitled to any military service pensions or benefits.

Charitas Hospital, Palembang Plaque

These words were chosen for the plaque for Charitas Hospital, to be placed next to the plaque to the military Prisoners of War:

> In loving memory of the men, women and children, internees of the Japanese between 1942 and 1945, who were treated in the Charitas Hospital, Palembang and with thanks for the bravery and skill of the nuns and doctors who cared for them.
> 'And there shall be no more death, neither sorrow nor crying, neither shall there be any more pain.' (Revelations 21:4)

Plaques were also prepared for the former men's camp in Muntok Jail, the former Muntok Women's Camp at Kampong Menjelang and a general plaque to remember all the internees, to be placed at the Tinwinning Building Museum.

The words for these plaques are as follows:

Men's camp in Muntok Jail:

> In loving memory of the civilian men and boys interned at Muntok by the Japanese between 1942 and 1945. They experienced sickness, starvation and often death but they showed great care for one another and courage in the face of such adversity.
> 'Who would true valour see, let him come hither.' (John Bunyan)

Women's camp at Kampong Menjelang, Muntok:

> In loving memory of the women and children interned in Muntok by the Japanese between 1942 and 1945. Civilians and Army Nurses were held captive here, experiencing hardship, ill-health and often

THE EVACUATION OF SINGAPORE

death. They cared for one another and shared the very little they had. Despite the squalor, they sought beauty in song:
'As blended voices filled the air,
The soul could soar to worlds more fair,
Escape from prison bounds'. (Margaret Dryburgh, camp internee)

The words of this plaque refer to the music transcribed from memory by Margaret Dryburgh and Norah Chambers, which was then rehearsed and sung by the Palembang women's vocal orchestra at the prison camp concerts. Both the singers and the audience were uplifted by the experience and were able to forget their degradation for a time. Many said the inspiring music gave them strength to survive.

Tinwinning Museum, Muntok:

> In loving memory of the men, women and children who suffered during the Japanese occupation between 1942 and 1945.
>
> Many were bombed and drowned in the Bangka Strait, others were killed in Muntok and many suffered deprivation, disease and death in internment camps.
>
> Their friends cared for them in the camps and in the Tinwinning Building hospital wards but many died and were buried in Muntok, Palembang and Loeboek Linggau and are now at rest.
> 'Their hearts were woven of human joys and cares,
> washed marvellously by sorrow' (Brooke)

The next step was to take the plaques to Palembang and Muntok. A second visit was arranged for February 2012, to coincide with the 70th anniversary of the fall of Singapore.

Former internee Ralph Armstrong and the Malayan Volunteers Group had put us in contact with Margie and Stephen Caldicott in England. Margie's grandmother, Mary Brown, and her mother, Shelagh Brown (later Mrs Lea), had been on board the *Vyner Brooke* and were then interned in the women's camps. Mrs Brown had died in Muntok, as had many of her and Shelagh's friends. After the war, Margie's mother had written to the British authorities for many years seeking maintenance of the Muntok graves, only to be told that civilian graves were not their responsibility.

I emailed Margie for some months and shared our stories. Anthony Pratt and I met the Caldicotts for the first time in Singapore – it was like greeting family.

The plaque in the Tinwinning Museum.

Singapore 2012, We Meet the Caldicotts, New Friends with Important Documents

Margie had brought with her a number of items that Anthony and I had not seen before and which were of immense help. She had a detailed map of the Muntok town (also known as the civil, old Dutch or European) cemetery. She also had lists of names of the British and Australians and the one New Zealander buried in the cemetery, with their plot and row numbers. The map and lists had been compiled by internees and the Dutch military at the end of the war. Margie's mother had annotated these lists of names, giving occupations, addresses and additional information.

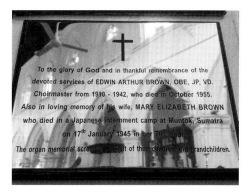

Plaque in St Andrew's Cathedral, Singapore, placed by Margie Caldicott's family in memory of her grandparents Edwin Arthur Brown, Cathedral Choirmaster, Changi and Sime Road internee, and Mary Brown, who died in Muntok Women's Camp.

In addition, Margie had brought with her copies of the photos taken of the Muntok cemetery by the visiting Indonesian religious minister in 1968, which showed a significant number of intact and upright crosses. This was definitely *not* a cemetery that had been fully emptied in 1964 but the resting place of many internees loved and remembered by their families!

70th Anniversary Ceremony of the Fall of Singapore, 2012

We travelled by bus with other Malayan Volunteers Group members to Singapore's Kranji War Cemetery for the service commemorating the fall of Singapore. This is held in mid-February each year. The year 2012 was an especially poignant one, commemorating the 70th anniversary of 15 February 1942, and a great many people attended.

We were very moved to see former Australian soldiers now in their late 80s. They were frail and walked with assistance or were in wheelchairs, but they moved slowly forward to place wreaths to their fallen comrades. Many soldiers had been prisoners of war in Changi or had been sent to work on the Burma Railway, where there was enormous loss of life. Civilian prisoners had been held separately in Changi and the Sime Road camps. These elderly soldiers who had given so much and had seen such sorrow, hardship and death were visibly affected and were quietly weeping; many observers were also wiping tears from their eyes.

The Japanese Ambassador to Singapore was present, laying a wreath and presenting 1,000 paper cranes made by schoolchildren, representing hope and peace.

THE EVACUATION OF SINGAPORE

Kranji War Cemetery, praying for peace, February 2012.

After speeches and wreath-laying, representatives of the many religions followed in Singapore stood together. A two-minute silence was held so that each person present could pray or hope for peace according to their own beliefs.

Charitas Hospital and Former Camp Sites, Palembang, February 2012

In Singapore, we met a party of Malayan Volunteers Group members who were travelling to Muntok by chartered boat, taking the original route of the evacuees from Singapore through the Malacca and Bangka Straits. We learned of their plans and arranged to meet in Muntok in several days' time.

From Singapore, Margie and Stephen Caldicott, Anthony Pratt and I flew to Palembang. At the Charitas Hospital, we were welcomed by our friends Professor Hardi Darmawan and the nursing nuns and by the Archbishop of Palembang, Aloysius Sudarso. We gathered in the boardroom of the hospital, which had been an operating theatre during the war years, still with original ceiling lights. We gave the memorial plaque to the hospital, explaining that we wished to thank the past staff for caring for our families during the war. The plaque will be placed next to the prisoner of war memorial in the foyer.

Margie had brought a photo of a young baby born to an internee at Charitas Hospital. The photo had been taken by a Japanese soldier who may have missed his own family at home. He had quietly passed the photo to the mother when she and her baby left the hospital to return to the women's prison camp.

Archbishop Sudarso was leaving that morning for a nine-hour drive to Lahat, near Lubuk Linggau, the site of our families' last internment camp. We asked if he would please say some prayers for the people who had suffered there during the war.

We enjoyed a traditional Indonesian morning tea at the hospital, with local delicacies such as pempek dumplings, before being taken on a tour. Charitas is a private hospital, but the fees of the paying patients support those who cannot pay. All patients receive the same excellent medical care, according to the creed of the Catholic Charitas Order. Charitas runs a number of hospitals and clinics in Sumatra, trains nursing and medical staff and operates schools.

A lovely and unexpected sight at the hospital was the nuns' museum. Here, in a small room, the story of the Charitas Order is told in a series of dioramas made from dolls dressed as nuns. The Charitas nuns had originally come from

Above left: Display representing the graves of nuns who died in Muntok and Bencoolen Prison Camps, Charitas Hospital Museum.

Above right: Foyer of Charitas Hospital with plaques from PoWs and the Malayan Volunteers Group.

the Netherlands in 1926 and first worked in Palembang in a small fourteen-bed hospital. The hospital has now grown to a large world-class facility.

One display in the museum explained the war year with dolls dressed as soldiers. Nearby were replicas of coffins of the two nuns who had died in Muntok prison camp and two who had died in Bencoolen camps. The four small dolls lay in lovingly arranged cardboard boxes, decorated with lace.

In Palembang, we again visited the area of Irenelaan, the former women's camp, which was situated in abandoned Dutch houses at Bukit Besar. The houses are still in use, with a small family or business occupying each two-bedroom home. During the war, around forty people were imprisoned in each house and more in the carport. The visit was an emotional one for Margie Caldicott, viewing the house where her mother and grandmother had lived.

There are no remnants of the former men's camp, which was nearby and was later lived in by the women. This camp had been made of bamboo and palm leaves, but the site is now covered by large new houses. Local people came out to speak to us, and one group told how they still see ghosts in their homes. They were not at all alarmed and seemed cheerful at describing this added company. I think we felt comforted to hear that the prisoners' houses are now inhabited by happy people who are not afraid of the dead.

Muntok, February 2012, All in the Same Family

The next day, we made the familiar ferry journey along the Moesi River to Muntok and were greeted by our kind friends from the Muntok Heritage Community. We met with the group who had travelled by boat from Singapore, tracing the path of the many thousands of evacuees who had left Singapore in February 1942. Also present was the family of Australian Army Nurse Carrie Jean Ashton, who had survived the prison camps.

THE EVACUATION OF SINGAPORE

With the Regent of Banka Barat and the jail director.

A convoy of cars drove us slowly to the home of Muntok's Regent, with headlights turned on as if in a funeral procession. We were welcomed by the Regent of Muntok and local people and escorted into the grounds under large decorative umbrellas. On the pillared porch, girls in beautiful mauve and gold costumes performed traditional dances to the beating of drums. Frangipani wreaths were placed around our necks, and we were invited to chew on a small smoking leaf.

After the welcoming ceremony, the Regent spoke to us all. He said that our ancestors had lived in Muntok at the same time as the ancestors of the local people and that because of this, we now all belong to the same family. He asked the local residents to respect the plaques we were about to place in memory of our relatives and all the prisoners once held in the camps. Anthony Pratt responded, thanking the Regent and the people of Muntok for their understanding, warmth and kindness.

A lovely meal on the verandah followed, and we again met Mr Afan, who was a boy in Muntok during the war. We were surprised to see he had a copy of Lavinia Warner's book about the camps, *Women in Captivity*.

The group then drove to Muntok Jail. Here we found that a black-tiled stand for the new plaque had been especially built in the garden outside the jail, near the front entrance. We presented the plaque, remembering the men and boys who had been imprisoned there during the war and the many who had perished.

From the jail, we drove to the site of the former women's camp at Kampong Menjelang. Here a green-tiled plinth had been built in the centre of the current village, near the old well that the women and children prisoners had used. This is the only remnant of the prison camp still visible. The Regent spoke again, explaining the plaque and asking the villagers to respect it.

The old well at Kampong Menjelang is still in use but does not provide enough water for the village. People must walk to a stream some distance away to bathe, wash clothes and obtain extra drinking water. Although Muntok is in a tropical area, there are serious droughts in the dry season. Margie, Stephen, Anthony and I decided to try to send donations to Muntok to contribute towards a new, deeper well and to help maintain the historic old well.

Women's Grave, Catholic Cemetery, Kampong Menjelang, Muntok

Our friends next drove us to the Catholic cemetery to see the grave that holds the '25 English people, victims of the Japanese war', reburied there after the building of the Pertamina petrol station in 1981.

REMEMBER ME

Margie Caldicott's plan of the old Dutch cemetery, prepared in 1948, showed us where the women who had died in Muntok Prison Camp had been reburied after the war. We could see on this plan that their reburied graves had lain exactly where the petrol tanks were later excavated and where the '25 English graves' had been found in 1981. It is thus a near certainty that these relocated graves in the Catholic cemetery contain the remains of the women internees who were not moved to Java. Thirty-six British and Australian women had died in Muntok Prison Camp, with three graves being moved to Java. After nearly forty years, it is to be expected that some of the remains were dislodged or taken by animals and not found.

Kampong Menjelang plaque.

We asked at the Catholic Church office in Santa Maria Church for any records of the reburial of the remains in 1981, hoping to find the names of those who were involved. Although the priest telephoned the main church office in Pangkalpinang, no additional details could be found.

Old Dutch Cemetery, Mr Herman and the Wall

We went once more to the site of the former town cemetery. The original entrance is still in place, to the right of the Pertamina petrol station on Muntok's main road. The two pillars of 1930s-style, crazy paving stones, very Dutch in appearance, mark the entry to Gang Durian or 'Durian Lane', an unmade path leading to a cluster of homes.

At the end of this lane, we met resident Mr Herman and his family in a pleasant house he built in the late 1960s. Mr Herman examined Margie's old cemetery photos taken in 1968 by the visiting church minister from Palembang. Prominent in the pictures can be seen a high, semicircular brick wall behind the remaining crosses. This was a memorial wall built by Dutch authorities in 1948, when they tidied the cemetery. It had stood behind the decorative wooden crosses that the Dutch had placed on the many rows of graves.

Mr Herman told us that he had pulled this wall down only a few years before to allow more light into his garden. He showed us exactly where it had been – and we were able to see the footprint of the original curved wall on the ground!

Abandoned cemetery and memorial wall, Muntok, 1968.

THE EVACUATION OF SINGAPORE

Likely location of my grandfather's grave.

Mr William, from another house behind the petrol station, took us into his garden to show us some tall, narrow concrete pillars that had formed the boundary of the cemetery. Several were still standing at the edge of his property and another lay on the ground.

Mrs Herman came from the house to help us, bringing drinks, folding chairs, a shady umbrella and a tape measure. Using Margie's cemetery map and lists of graves, we were able to measure the likely locations of each man's grave. My grandfather's remains probably lie in the garden of an adjoining home, in a bed growing vegetables and herbs and with chickens pecking on the ground.

Anthony Pratt's father's grave lies in the yard of a house nearby. More residents came from their homes to assist us. The owner of the property where my grandfather's grave lies told of finding human remains when digging the foundations for his house in the late 1960s.

Despite the frustration of knowing our families' graves had been so neglected by British and Australian authorities, I was happy to see children playing and the chickens scratching near my grandfather's grave. I was glad to know he was buried near his friends and that he was now surrounded by happiness and activity rather than lying in an unmarked and 'unknown' war grave far away in Jakarta.

I was reminded of the poem by Caribbean judge H.D. Carberry:

> I shall lie in the rich, moist earth
> Of the forked-up flower bed someday, Oh put no stone above my head
> I would be earth I say…
>
> So lay me in my narrow bed, And let me be,
> With no stone at my head, No narrow box about me,
> But in the earth beneath the stars I would be free

Teluk Menggeris or Inggris, English Bay

The following day, motor boats carried us again to Radji Beach, also known as English Bay. We travelled parallel to the shoreline – the ride was gentle and undulating and the spray and refreshing wind cooled our skin. We waded ashore through the clear water. The sand was crisply white and tall palms rustled. It was a postcard scene of a tropical holiday.

However, this had not been a restful place seventy years before. We thought of the massacre of the Australia Army nurses, civilians, two groups of servicemen and the stretcher cases by Japanese soldiers here on 16 February 1942. This had been fully documented by the three survivors, Nurse Vivian Bullwinkel, Ernest Lloyd, a stoker from the *Prince of Wales*, and American Brewer Eric Germann, all from the *Vyner Brooke*.

Terrified local villagers had fled their homes, never to return. The harsh and senseless killings, horrendous in any setting, seemed doubly out of place in these beautiful surroundings. We again gathered pebbles to take home for the families of these nurses while our own hurt and confusion was eased by the kindness of our Indonesian friends.

Remembering the Lost Graves of Muntok

In Muntok, we were again aware that most of the civilians who died there had no memorial. We decided to prepare a plaque with the names of the civilians who had died in in the Muntok camps, as shown in Margie's lists and whom we believe remain buried there. As mentioned, all Dutch military and civilian graves, those of the Australian Army nurses and a small number of British and Australian civilian graves had been moved to Java in 1964, but the vast majority of British, Australian and New Zealand civilian graves had been left behind in Muntok, forgotten by their countries but not by their families.

We also resolved to send contributions to Muntok and to Charitas Hospital in Palembang to help with health, education and welfare. We wanted to assist the local communities and remember the prisoners. In this way, our families would not be forgotten and some good finally could follow, despite their deaths.

Margie Caldicott, a flautist and flute teacher, decided to help plan a concert in England using the music of the original women's vocal orchestra, first sung in Palembang Camp in 1943. Her mother and grandmother had been camp choir members, and her mother had brought her music scores home after the war. The music had been performed in the USA, the Netherlands and Australia and was featured in the Australian film *Paradise Road* but had not yet been sung publicly in the United Kingdom. The planned concert would aim to raise funds to help the people in Muntok and to raise money towards the new plaque. We would also try once more to increase British and Australian governments' awareness of Muntok's 'lost graves'.

The following is a list of British, Australian and New Zealand civilian internees who died in Muntok and whose graves were, for the most part, *not* moved to Java in 1964. The graves of the Australian nurses who died in camp were moved to the Menteng Pulo war cemetery in Jakarta because they were military personnel. The graves of the crew of the *Empress of Asia*, employees of Cable and Wireless and a small number of civilians from the police force or other services were also moved to Java and a small number by their families. But all others were left behind in the

THE EVACUATION OF SINGAPORE

Muntok cemetery to be built over, or, in the case of the women, moved to a group grave in the Catholic cemetery during building of the petrol station in 1981.

Sadly, the bodies of the nurses, civilian men and women and servicemen killed on Radji Beach and that of Mr Vivian Bowden were never found. The following people remain buried in Muntok today with no named or identifiable graves.

British and Australian Civilian Internee Women Who Died in Muntok

These women were buried by their friends under rubber trees near Kampong Menjelang Prison Camp. Their bodies were moved to the Muntok town cemetery by Dutch authorities at the end of the Second World War and believed to be reburied in either one or three communal graves in Muntok Catholic cemetery in 1981:

(Name/age/date of death) 33 graves
Mrs Theresia 'Resie' Armstrong (51), 7 February 1945
Miss Dixie Armstrong (32), 5 April 1945
Mrs Mary Awmack Battensby (51), 11 February 1945
Mrs Edith Florence Bedell (65), 19 January 1945
Mrs Mary Elizabeth Brown (67), 17 January 1945
Mrs Edith Evangeline Castle (50), 19 November 1944
Mrs Mary Louise Day (53), 16 December 1944
Mrs Helen Dixey (48), 28 February 1945
Mrs Agnes Gertrude Dominguez (63), 9 November 1944
Mrs Marjory Gray (55), 13 January 1945
Mrs Muriel Gregory (43), 5 November 1944
Mrs Rena Rosie Haynes (49), 10 January 1945
Mrs Kathleen Mary Hutchings (46), 1 2 April 1945
Mrs Blanche Lucy Jones (58), 8 December 1944
Miss Sabine Elizabeth Mackintosh (57), 27 December 1944
Mrs Dorothy MacLeod (59), 1 April 1945
Mrs Joan May Maddams (36), 19 December 1944
Mrs Evelyn Mary Parr (38), 11 January 1945
Mrs Isobel Veronica 'Mo' Pennefather (48), 15 March 1945
Mrs Sylvia Plummer (42), 19 November 1944
Miss Eva Prouse (49), 2 February 1945
Mrs Lillian Rodrigues (46), 1 January 1945
Mrs Ruth Russell-Roberts (36), 20 January 1945
Mrs Amy Alexandra Mary Simmons (30), 26 February 1945
Mrs Louise Sinnatt (32), 23 February 1945
Mrs Esme Barbara Skinner (38), 27 March 1945
Mrs Emily Elizabeth Smith (72), 9 November 1944
Mrs Nellie Ellen Tay (40), 21 November 1944

REMEMBER ME

Miss Lottie Regina Wales (48), 3 January 1945
Mrs Marion Galloway Langdon Williams (46), 7 February 1945
Mrs Cevia Deitch Warman (25), 9 March 1942 (died in the coolie lines)

British, Australian and New Zealand Men Who Died in Muntok Jail and who are believed to remain in Muntok

These men were buried by their friends in the Muntok town (old Dutch or civil) cemetery. Their graves were not moved by their own countries and are now believed to have been built over by houses and the Pertamina petrol station.

(Name/age/date of death) 57 graves
Mr C.H. Adam, 5 October 1944
Mr Frederick Marshall Adam (38), 25 January 1945, ARP, Singapore
Mr John C.H. Aitken (54), 25 November 1944, LDC
Mr Charles John Arnold (70), 9 June 1944, MSVR
Mr L.R. Blake (47), 23 February 1945, RNVR
Mr F.V. Boswell (51), 10 July 1944
Mr Francis Grainger Brown (44), 5 November 1944
Mr Lindsay Burn (58), 8 November 1944
Mr Thomas Burns (50), 22 October 1944
Mr Gordon Burt O.B.E. (46), 28 January 1945,
Mr Colin Douglas Campbell (53), 2 August 1944, MSVR
Sir John Bruce Stuart Campbell (66), 14 October 1943, WW1 Croix de Guerre
Mr Richard James Potter Clarke (56), 19 November 1944
Mr Vernon Rowe Connolly (49), 17 October 1944
Mr John Gallagher Dominguez (65), 11 September 1944
Mr Kenneth Godfrey Arthur Dohoo (38), 25 October 1944
Mr Walter Pattinson Douglas (55), 23 November 1944
Mr E.A.M. Dumas, 1 December 1944
Mr Thomas Efford (59), 24 November 1944
Mr Michael Francis Enright (63), 24 January 1945, RVNR
Mr David Richard Evans (60), 30 July 1944
Mr John Samuel Evans (37), 17 July 1944
Mr Frederick Fletcher (70), 9 June 1944
Mr George Basil Warburton Gray (62), 12 February 1944
Mr Cecil Reynold Grixoni (43), 28 October 1944
Mr George Henry Hallam, 18 July 1944
Mr Geoffrey Holderness (45), 28 May 1944
Mr Leslie Gordon B. Jeffrey (53), 2 May 1944
Mr Charles Martin Jenkin (51), 17 November 1944
Mr Algernon Neville Laybourne (54), 28 July 1944
Mr Frederick Langharne Llewellyn (48), 13 May 1944

THE EVACUATION OF SINGAPORE

Mr E.H.M. Manden, (23), July 1944
Mr John McGuffin (52), 8 March 1945
Mr Robert Meldrum (49), 13 December 1944
Mr Jack Stephenson Messenger (45), 2 November 1944
Mr Riley Llewellyn Morgan (47), 20 July 1944,
Mr Robert Wallace Morris (42), 8 June 1944, SSVF
Mr Walter Penrice (47), 20 July 1944
Mr Richard Henry Cozens Prior (61), 15 August 1944
Mr Donald Frederick Pratt (37), 1 May 1945, Johore Volunteer Engineers
Mr Vincent Bristow Pybus (57), 11 November 1944
Mr C.G. Rebel, 10 November 1944
Mr Gordon Stanley Reis (55), 2 November 1944
Mr Joseph Sharpe-Elliott, (55), 4 July 1944
Mr G.C. Spandaw, 30 May 1944
Mr James Henry Stanners (32), 22 January 1945
Mr Robert Stephenson (47), 8 April 1945
Mr Reginald Joseph Strong, (55), 21 February 1945
Mr Frederick Thompson (36), 27 November 1944
Mr Henry Stanley Tisshaw (56), 24 November 1944
Mr W. Vorlauf (54), 5 February 1945
Reverend Albert Victor Wardle (47), 4 January 1945
Mr Harry Leonard Watson (31), 2 November 1944
Mr Hubert Victor Miles Woods (43), 21 November 1943
Mr Thomas Kinnear Wilson (53), 22 November 1944
Mr Alfred Herbert Wright (44), 9 February 1945
Mr Herbert Zimmerman (43), 11 June 1944

Mr Vivian Gordon Bowden (57), Australia's Official Representative to Singapore, killed by 2 guards outside the Muntok cinema. His grave, dug by Mr Bowden, is believed to lie behind the cinema.

Locations of Graves in former Muntok Town/Civil/Old Dutch Cemetery

These men buried here now lie under houses and the Pertamina petrol station.

Plot 1 Row D No 2 Mr Algernon Neville Laybourne
Plot 1 Row D No 5 Mr Michael Francis Enright
Plot 1 Row D No 6 Sir John Bruce Stuart Campbell
Plot 1 Row D No 8 Mr G.C. Spandaw
Plot 1 Row D No 9 Mr L.G. Jeffrey
Plot 1 Row D No 10 Mr George Basil Warburton Gray
Plot 1 Row D No 12 Mr Hubert Victor Miles Woods

REMEMBER ME

Plot 1 Row D No 13 Mr G. Holderness
Plot 1 Row D No 14 Mr Robert Wallace Morris
Plot 1 Row D No 15 Mr Frederick Fletcher
Plot I Row D No 16 Mr Frederick Langharne Llewellyn
Plot 1 Row D No 18 Mr Charles John Arnold
Plot 1 Row E No 1 Mr F.V. Boswell
Plot 1 Row E No 2 Mr George Henry Hallam
Plot 1 Row E No 3 Mr John Samuel Evans
Plot 1 Row E No 5 Mr Walter Penrice
Plot 1 Row E No 6 Mr David Richard Evans
Plot 1 Row E No 7 Colin Douglas Campbell
Plot 1 Row E No 11 Francis Grainger Brown
Plot 1 Row E No 12 Vincent Bristow Pybus
Plot 1 Row E No 13 Mr Robert Stephenson
Plot 1 Row E No 14 Mr W. Vorlauf
Plot 1 Row E No 15 Mr Donald Frederick Pratt
Plot 1 Row E No 16 Mr James Henry Stanners
Plot 1 Row E No 17 Mr John C. Aitken
Plot 1 Row E No 19 Mr Riley Lewellyn Morgan
Plot 1 1 Row E No 21 Mr John McGuffin
Plot 1 Row E No 22 Mr Gordon Burt
Plot 1 Row E No 23 Mr C.H. Adam
Plot 1 Row E No 24 Mr L.R. Blake
Plot 1 Row E No 26 Mr Alfred Herbert Wright
Plot 1 Row E No 27 Mr Herbert Zimmerman
Plot 1 Row F No 2 Reverend Vic Wardle
Plot 1 Row F No 3 Robert Meldrum
Plot 1 Row F No 4 Mr F. Thompson
Plot 1 Row F No 6 Mr G. Reis
Plot 1 Row F No 7 Mr H.S. Tisshaw
Plot 1 Row F No 8 Mr T. Efford
Plot 1 Row F No 9 Mr W.P. Douglas
Plot 1 Row F No 10 Mr R.J.P. Clarke
Plot 1 Row F No 11 Mr T.K. Wilson
Plot 1 Row F No 12 Mr H.L. Watson
Plot 1, Row F No 13 Charles Martin Jenkin
Plot 1 Row F No 16 Mr C.G. Rebel
Plot 1 Row F No 17 Mr L. Burn
Plot 1 Row F No 20 Mr C.R. Grixoni
Plot 1 Row F No 21 Mr G.A. Dohoo
Plot 1 Row F No 22 Mr T. Burns
Plot 1 Row F No 23 Mr V.B. Connelly
Plot 1 Row F No 26 Mr J.G. Dominguez
Plot 1 Row F No 27 Mr R.H. Prior

THE EVACUATION OF SINGAPORE

Plot 1 Row H No 20 Mr E.H.M. Manden
Plot 1 Row 1 No 27 Mr E.A.G.A. Dumas
And Mr Frederick Marshall Adam, Mr John Sharpe Elliott and Mr Reginald Strong

The women were initially buried in Kampong Menjelang Camp, reburied in this former cemetery by Dutch authorities after the war and then moved to the civilian grave, Muntok Catholic cemetery, in 1981.

Plot 3 Row J No 7 Mrs Mary Louise Day
Plot 3 Row J No 8 Mrs Marjory Gray
Plot 3 Row J No 9 Mrs Rena Rosie Haynes
Plot 3 Row J No 10 Mrs Resie Armstrong
Plot 3 Row J No 11 Mrs Louise Sinnatt
Plot 3 Row K No 7 Mrs Esme Barbara Skinner
Plot 3 Row K No 8 Mrs Amy Alexandra Mary Simmons
Plot 3 Row K No 9 Mrs Edith Florence Bedell
Plot 3 Row K No 10 Mrs Mary Elizabeth Brown
Plot 3 Row K No 11 Mrs Helen Dixey
Plot 3 Row L No 7 Mrs Lilian Rodrigues
Plot 3 Row L No 8 Mrs Agnes Dominguez
Plot 3 Row L No 9 Mrs Marion Galloway
Plot 3 Row L No 10 Mrs Dorothy Macleod
Plot 3 Row M No 7 Mrs Evelyn Mary Parr
Plot 3 Row M No 8 Mrs Edith Evangeline Castle
Plot 3 Row M No 9 Miss Eva Prouse
Plot 3 Row M No 10 Miss Dixie Resie Armstrong
Plot 3 Row M No 11 Mrs Kathleen Mary Hutchings
Plot 3 Row N No 7 Mrs Olga Mary Neubronner
Plot 3 Row N No 8 Mrs Mary Awmack Battensby
Plot 3 Row N No 9 Mrs Isobel Veronica Pennefather

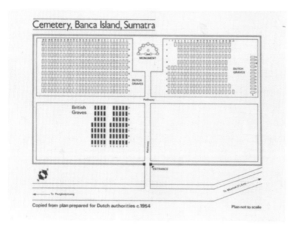

Mislabelled, British men's graves to left rear, British women's graves left front, Dutch graves right rear.

Plot 3 Row N No 10 Mrs Emily Elizabeth Smith
Plot 3 Row O No 7 Miss Lottie Regina Reginald Wales
Plot 3 Row O No 8 Mrs Joan May Maddams
Plot 3 Row O No 9 Mrs Ruth Russell-Roberts
Plot 3 Row O No 11 Mrs Muriel Gregory
Plot 3 Row P No 7 Miss Sabine Elizabeth MacKintosh
Plot 3 Row P No 8 Mrs Blanch Lucy Jones
Plot 3 Row P No 9 Mrs Nellie Ellen Tay
Plot 3 Row P No 10 Mrs Sylvia Plummer
And Mrs Marjorie Hindaugh Cocke
And Mrs Claire Sammy
And Mrs C. Warman

British Men Who Died in Muntok Jail But Whose Graves Were Moved to Java Around 1961 (Because of Their Past Occupations, Involving Uniform)

Mr Ernest Henry Tunn, 13 January 1944, Chief Inspector of Police, Malacca
Mr Herbert Smallwood, 29 March 1944, kitchen porter, *Empress of Asia*
Mr George Oliver Roberts, 16 June 1944, assistant architect, sergeant ISSVF (uniformed officer in Volunteer Forces)
Mr Thomas Henry Roberts, 25 June 1944, waiter and merchant seaman, *Empress of Asia*
Mr Richard Frederick Lionel La Nauze, 28 July 1944, Cable and Wireless radio broadcasting
Mr John Sharpe Elliot, 4 July 1944, Public Works Department and naval base engineer
Mr Willian A. Nesfield, 2 August 1944, Harbour Board, Penang
Mr William James Marlow, 11 August 1944, waiter, *Empress of Asia*
Mr George Bate Edmund Truscott, 12 August 1944, Merchant Navy
Mr William Tickle, 8 September 1944, assistant engineer
Mr Ralph Samuel St George Johnston, 6 October 1944, captain in Selangor LDC (Volunteer Forces)
Mr Philip Christian Barnes, 7 November 1944, Singapore LDC (Volunteer Forces)
Mr Bernard Medlicott Bree, 14 November 1944, *Empress of Asia*
Mr Harry Ernest Monk Mason, 15 November 1944, Perak LDC (Volunteer Forces)
Mr Alexander Park Cranna, 4 January 1945, planter and sergeant Selangor LDC (Volunteer Forces)
Mr Hugh Brown Sym, 10 January 1945, Assistant Superintendent of Police, Singapore
Mr Neil Seward Killick, 11 January 1945, planter and member Selangor LDC (Volunteer Forces)
Mr Salvatore Stellini, 21 January 1945, Merchant Navy
Mr Thomas Abraham Curran-Sharp, 4 February 1945, private in Selangor LDC (Volunteer Forces)

THE EVACUATION OF SINGAPORE

British Women Whose Graves Were Moved from Muntok to Java, 1961

Mrs Claire Sammy, 18 November 1944, husband a judge in Singapore
Mrs Olga Neubronner, 2 March 1945, in charge of St John's Ambulance, Singapore
Mrs Marjorie Hindaugh Cocke, 5 March 1945, worked for St John's Ambulance

Twelve Australian Army Nurses Believed Killed in Bombing of SS *Vyner Brooke* or Washed Away on Rafts (or Possibly Murdered Elsewhere)

Louvinia Bates (32)
Ellenor Calnan (29)
Mary Clarke (30)
Millicent Dorsch (29)
Caroline Ennis (28)
Kathleen (Kit) Kinsella (37)
Gladys McDonald (32)
Olive Paschke (36)
Lavinia Jean Russell (32)
Marjorie Schuman (31)
Annie Trenerry (32)
Mona Wilton (28)

Twenty-One Australian Army Nurses from *SS Vyner Brooke* Killed on Radji Beach on 16 February 1942 and Who Have No Known Graves

Elaine Balfour Ogilvy (30)
Alma Beard (29)
Ada Bridge (34)
Florence (Flo) Casson (38)
Mary Cuthbertson (31)
Irene Drummond (36)
Dorothy (Bud) Elmes (27)
Lorna Fairweather (29)
Peggy Farmaner (28)
Nancy Harris (29)
Clarice Halligan (37)
Minnie Hodgson (33)
Ellen Louisa (Nell) Keats (26)
Janet (Jenny) Kerr (31)

Mary Eleanor (Ellie) McGlade (39)
Kathleen Neuss (30)
Florence Salmon (26)
Jean Stewart (37)
Mona Tait (27)
Bessie Wilmot (28)
Rosetta Wight (33)

Four Australian Army Nurses from SS *Vyner Brooke* Died in Muntok Women's Camp, Later Moved to Commonwealth War Graves Cemetery in Jakarta

Wilhelmina (Mina) Raymont (33), 8 February 1945
Irene Singleton (36), 20 February 1945
Pauline Blanche Hempsted (36) 19 March 1945
Dora Shirley Gardam (34), 4 April 1945

Four Australian Army Nurses from SS *Vyner Brooke* Died in Belalau Women's Camp, Later Moved to Commonwealth War Graves Cemetery in Jakarta

Gladys Hughes (36), 31 March 1945
Winnie Davis (30), 19 July 1945
Rubina Dorothy (Dot) Freeman (30), 8 August 1945
Pearl (Mitz) Mittelheuser (41), 18 August 1945

A memorial bench has been placed by families in the Menteng Pulo Cemetery in Jakarta, overlooking the adjoining Commonwealth War Graves cemetery where the eight nurses who died in camp are buried.

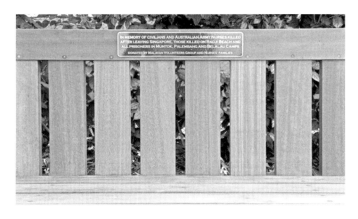

Memorial Bench, Menteng Pulo Cemetery, Jakarta.

THE EVACUATION OF SINGAPORE

Nursing and Medical Staff in Muntok, Palembang and Belalau Prison Camps, not including Australian Army Nurses

Women's Camp
Edith Florence Bedell, Nurse, died 19/1/1945, (65), Muntok
Phyllis Briggs, Nurse
Rachel Brooks, Nurse
Edith Castle, Colonial Nursing Sister, died 19/11/1944, (50), Muntok
Marjorie Hindaugh Cocke, St John's Ambulance Volunteer, died 5/3/1945, (53), Muntok
Marjorie Cooke, Nurse
Mary Cooper, QA Nursing Sister (Queen Alexandra Imperial Military Nursing Service), died 20/6/1945, (27), Belalau
Jessie Coupland, Nurse, Malayan Nursing Service
Joy Dexter, Health visitor, Women and Children's clinic
Ruth Dickson, QA Nursing Sister (Queen Alexandra Imperial Military Nursing Service), died 24/12/1944, (54), Muntok
M. Dlish, Nurse
Dr Annamaria Curth-Goldberg, physician and paediatrician
Mary Jenkin, Medical Auxiliary Service, died 16/8/1945, (49), Belalau
Marjorie Jennings, Nurse, died 12/5/1945 (37), Belalau
K.E. Kong, Nurse
Janet Macalister, Nurse
Helen Mackenzie, Nurse
Freda Mackinnon, Assistant Matron, Penang General Hospital
Mary McCallum, Nurse
Jean McDowell, Doctor
Rennie McFie, Nurse, died 14/6/1945, (50), Belalau
Olga Neubronner, Colonial Service Nurse, St John's Ambulance, Singapore, died 22/3/1945, (39), Muntok
Sally Oldham, Nurse, died 19/6/1944, (51), Palembang
Joan Powell, Nurse
Violet Pulford, Nurse
Alice Rossie, Nurse
Ruth Russell Roberts, Medical Auxiliary Service Ambulance driver, died 18/1/1945, (36), Muntok
Hyda Scott-Eames, Medical Auxiliary Service Nurse, died 13/4/1945, (42), in train near Palembang
Constance Smith, Surgeon, Women and Children's welfare officer
Netta Smith, Nurse
Phyllis Thane, Voluntary Aid Detachment Nurse
Margaret Thompson, Doctor
Margot Turner, QA Nursing Sister (Queen Alexandra Imperial Military Nursing Service)
40 Catholic Nuns, of whom Sr. M. Agnesia and Sr. M. Gemma died in Muntok Camp

REMEMBER ME

Men's Camp
Harley Clark, Dentist (Men's Camp)
Dr Lentze (former director Pangkalpinang Hospital) (Men's Camp)
Albert McKern Doctor (Men's Camp), died 16/6/1945, (62), Belalau
Hugh Stubbs, Doctor (Men's Camp)
Dr Tay (Men's Camp)
George (Paddy) West, Doctor (Men's Camp)
Father Benedictus Bakker and 11 Catholic Brothers who died while caring for dysentery patients

And Dutch Nurses and Doctors and others whose names we do not know

How Men Die

>Quiet Night Thoughts
>
>Before my bed,
>There is bright moonlight,
>So that it seems
>Like frost on the ground.
>
>Lifting my head,
>I watch the bright moon:
>Lowering my head,
>I dream that I am home.
>
>   Li Po, 701–762 AD

Aerial photos from the 1930s in the Timah Tinwinning Museum show the exact location of the former coolie lines (public works depot) next to Muntok Jail and connected to it by a barbed wire run. Men were taken from the jail into this rudimentary 'hospital' to be nursed and to die. Here the men lay on concrete slabs, naked or covered by a hessian sack, starved, fevered with malaria, choked and bloated with beriberi or flooded with dysentery faeces.

There were named wards for each illness but no medicine to treat the conditions. The men were cared for by their tireless friends and the Catholic brothers

Muntok Jail.

who volunteered to work in the dysentery ward. Eleven brothers died doing this dangerous work. Doctors and helpers worked constantly, cleaning the men's bodies, offering sips of rice gruel and trying to comfort them. There was no quinine for malaria, no vitamins or nourishing food, so only supportive treatment could be given.

Camp records from internee Jock Brodie's memoirs show the following numbers of deaths for the men in Muntok Jail from June to December 1944. At times, there were up to six deaths per day:

June (14)
July (23)
August (21)
September (14)
October (30)
November (58)
December (33)

These figures represent an enormous mortality rate from diseases that should have been prevented by adequate food and living conditions or cured with suitable care. Similar death rates occurred in Muntok Women's Camp.

William McDougall worked day and night caring for patients in this 'hospital', stopping only to document the names of the dead. The Japanese provided him with a typewriter and insisted that records of each death be kept. After the war, his experiences led him to enter a seminary, becoming a priest and then a monsignor in Utah, USA, and to write about these tragic times.

By June 1944, nearly 1,000 men were held captive in Muntok Jail and adjacent 'hospital'. Food supplies were pitiful and medicines non-existent. There were no longer any birds singing – they had all been caught and eaten.

The British and Dutch camp leaders repeatedly asked the Japanese for more food and medicines – instead, the Japanese removed the scales that had been used to measure and document the men's weight each month. The scales, in fact, were not necessary – it was evident to the naked eye that the men were underfed and skeletal.

In his post-war memoirs, internee Jock Brodie wrote that: 'Muntok was a tragedy to the men and women of both camps. The hundreds of graves provide the evidence of the callous and barbaric institution of the Japanese authority.'

There were indeed hundreds of internees' graves in Muntok, but they were not preserved and there was no official memorial. News of the opening in 2013 of the Timah Tinwinning Building Museum with the Vivian Bullwinkel Galleri documenting the Japanese invasion of Muntok was indeed very welcome.

REMEMBER ME

The Timah Tinwinning Building Museum, Muntok

The Timah Tinwinning Building Museum opened in 2013 under Director Mr Fakhrizal Abubakar. The museum has wonderful technical displays showing the history of tin mining on Bangka Island. At the front of the museum is the 'The Vivian Bullwinkel Galleri' dedicated to the Second World War. Here, newspapers, photographs and artefacts depict the events of the war as it struck Muntok in February 1942. Cabinets hold pictures of the bombing of the ships in the Bangka Strait, reports of the Radji Beach massacre and Australian Army nurses' and Japanese uniforms. These items were donated by prisoners' families.

A display relates the story of Mr Vivian Bowden, Australia's Official Representative to Singapore, who was killed by two guards in Muntok on 17 February 1942, the only Australian ambassador to have died in time of war.

The museum library houses editions of William McDougall's diaries, published as *If I Get out Alive* and his books *By Eastern Windows* and *Six Bells off Java*, Betty Jeffrey's recollections of camp life in *White Coolies*, Pat Gunther's *Diary of a Nurse* and Lavinia Warner's *Women Beyond the Wire*, together with bound copies of the diaries of internees Gordon Reis, Jock Brodie and others. Here visitors may read and learn about the prison camps, the neglect and harsh treatment of the prisoners and their bravery and fortitude. A thousand people visited the museum in its first three months of opening.

Mr Agung Purnama, Timah Tinwinning Museum guide.

Examining the Past

Historians from the Muntok Heritage Community and others wished to know more about the prison camps and how our families had been affected. Local people had also experienced bombing, death, assault, fear and food shortage during the war. It is difficult to know how to portray the period of the Second World War sensitively, giving due attention to its horrors but without distressing families of prisoners and the people who live in Muntok. Lives of men, women and children were altered irrevocably during the Japanese occupation. Many died, leaving families to suffer, while survivors and their descendants carried terrible memories and knowledge.

Our own families frequently did not know the fate of their relatives for a considerable time, if ever. Records of those on board the bombed boats were scant or not kept at all in the panic of leaving Singapore. Many on board were presumed dead in the resulting chaos. Passenger and crew lists are now being reconstructed painstakingly from diaries and archival sources by Malayan Volunteers Group Historian Michael Pether in New Zealand.

The Red Cross visited the Palembang camps in 1942, asking prisoners to fill out cards with last sightings of missing people. It later tried to obtain details of all internees from those who survived the war. As late as 1947, newspapers carried advertisements seeking information. The following query from the Imperial War Graves Commission shows that for some families the period of waiting to learn their loved ones' fate was agonisingly long – in these cases, over two years after the end of war. Many families and friends had delayed closure, while for some this has not yet occurred.

The West Australian, Perth, 8 September 1947

CIVILIAN DEATHS IN WAR, Commission Seeks More Information
A list of civilians who died during World War II while internees in Japanese occupied territory has been forwarded by the Imperial War Graves Commission. Additional information about the deceased, whose next-of-kin are believed to be in Australia, is sought by the commission in order to complete its records. Next-of-kin are asked

EXAMINING THE PAST

to communicate with the commission's Australian headquarters at 434 Collins Street, Melbourne.

The following is the list of civilians who died in Japanese occupied territory, showing the date of death and the place of burial where known:

Dominguez, J.G., September 11, 1944.
Dominquez, Agnes, November 9, 1944.
Enright, Michael Francis, June 1945, South Sumatra.
La Nauze, R.F.L., July 28, 1944.
Lewis A.A., September 2, 1945, Padang.
Meldrum, Robert, December 13, 1944, Sumatra camp.
Nesfield, William Arthur, August 2, 1944, South Sumatra.
Robins, Hubert Harry, April 1942.
Pratt, Donald Frederick, May 1, 1945, South Sumatra.
Reis, Gordon Stanley, December 2, 1944, South Sumatra.
Skinner Mrs. Esme, March 22, 1945.
Tongue, Edwin, March 22, 1945, Pom Pong Island.
Watts-Carter, Mrs. Millicent, August 27, 1945.
Weir, Hugh Loudown, July 16, 1944.
Wood, the Rev. G. November 12, 1944.

Many of these people listed above had died in Muntok surrounded by their friends and fellow internees. They had named graves, and records of their deaths had been carefully recorded in camp. Yet by 1947, the authorities did not have an exact record of where the deaths had taken place and some families had not yet been informed. Adding to this indignity, the graves of those who died in Muntok had not been cared for by their own countries and the deceased were repeatedly denied a memorial.

Above left: Old Muntok pier leading to customs house and cinema, 1930s.

Above right: Aerial photo of Muntok, 1930s, rectangular jail at bottom left. Tinwinning Building (now Timah Museum) adjacent and above.

Chichester, October 2013

Margaret Dryburgh and Norah Chambers, founders of the Palembang women's prison camp vocal orchestra.

> Assembled spirits far and wide
> Unite with brilliance
> Shine among us day and night
> Sing in patterns and frame the dead
>   Eira Day, daughter of child internee Harry Dyne

Singing to Survive Concert, St Paul's Church, Chichester, 26 October 2013

The work to remember those killed after leaving Singapore and the internees, particularly those who died in camp and now lie buried in 'Muntok's lost graves', continued.

After her visit to Muntok in 2012, Margie Caldicott joined a dedicated committee to produce a concert featuring the music of the original women's prison

CHICHESTER, OCTOBER 2013

camp vocal orchestra. This had been first sung in Palembang Women's Camp on 27 December 1943 and in several following concerts, and it gave the women and children vital support. The planned concert in Chichester aimed to tell of the fortitude of the women internees, who had included Margie's mother and grandmother, and how the music had been able to lift the women from despair. The audience would now hear this music publicly performed in England for the first time.

Proceeds from the concert would be sent to Muntok to help a community project and would pay for a plaque with the names of the British, Australian and New Zealand civilian internees who had died in Muntok and are still buried there. Sadly, by contrast, all the Dutch civilian internees' graves had been moved to war cemeteries in Java after the war. In October 2013, I travelled to England to attend the concert and to meet old and new friends. Now, after months of preparation, the concert was about to start.

We sat quietly in St Paul's Church, Chichester, waiting for the audience to assemble and for the concert to begin. The plaster walls and simple décor made a fitting venue for this humble and stirring occasion. The church was soon full, as over 400 people gathered to hear the choral music first sung seventy years ago.

Looking around, we saw the many families and friends of the prisoners, who could each tell a different story. There were three ladies present who had been interned as children. They wore a corsage of a red rose as a tribute to their courage in attending the evening and so we could identify and greet them.

Family members of the original choir were present – relatives of Dorothy Macleod, who had the most wonderful voice and was one of many who had died, the family of Shelagh and Mrs Mary Brown and relations of Australian Army Nurse Betty Jeffrey.

The audience came from far afield. Betty Jeffrey's niece and great-niece had travelled from Australia. They wore Betty's army medals, earnt at such a cost. The son and family of Hal Hammett, the British men's camp leader, came from Jersey in the Channel Islands. Other internees' families came from many parts of the United Kingdom and some from the USA. One lady had only heard about the concert from Margie Caldicott's radio interview that week and had not known beforehand where her relatives had been imprisoned and died.

In the camp, two women captives, Margaret Dryburgh and Norah Chambers, had transcribed classical music from memory and taught the thirty women who joined the prison camp choir. The women were of many nationalities, speaking a variety of languages. The music had been arranged so the choir could make sounds with their voices rather than singing with unfamiliar words.

Weakened through sickness and hunger and unable to stand, the original choir members had sat on boxes or small stools as they sang. The music performed in the prison camp offered unexpected beauty and consolation to the otherwise degraded prisoners, creating a mental escape from their terrible surroundings. Even the harsh guards had been stunned into silence at the wonder of the songs.

Later, when their living conditions deteriorated and many were dying from disease and starvation, the memory of the vocal orchestra continued to offer the women comfort and some freedom from mental torment.

THE EVACUATION OF SINGAPORE

We were assembled now to listen to the wonderful music. As we waited, we remembered the thousands fleeing Singapore whose boats were bombed and who died at sea. We recalled the men, women and children who suffered in the camps and the many who did not survive. We thought, too, of all who suffer in dreadful wars today.

Seated in the church, I recalled the words from the Bible, from 2 Corinthians 1:8; written 2,000 years ago, they aptly describe the prisoners' suffering:

> We think you ought to know, dear brothers and sisters, about the trouble we went through in the province of Asia. We were crushed and overwhelmed beyond our ability to endure, and we thought we would never live through it.

And indeed, so many did not survive, with half of the men and one third of the women dying in camp.

Photographs of Norah Chambers and Margaret Dryburgh looked down on us from the nave. The audience was silent as the choir, dressed in black, entered the church. We were moved to see that as a mark of respect to the prisoners, the choir members wore no shoes...

The narration for the concert was written by Lavinia Warner and the event filmed by her for future researchers. A film producer, Lavinia had interviewed English nurse and camp survivor Brigadier Dame Margot Turner and her fellow internees some years ago for an episode of *This is Your Life*. Lavinia later visited Sumatra with Margot Turner and Australian Nurse Betty Jeffrey, making a documentary, *Women in Captivity*, about the prisoners' experiences.

Inspired by this work and by meeting many former prisoners in the 1980s, Lavinia Warner and John Sandilands wrote the detailed book about the women's camp, *Women Beyond the Wire*. Mr Afan, our friend in Muntok, had a treasured copy of this book in his home. Lavinia subsequently produced the long-running TV series *Tenko* about female internees of the Japanese – she was thus extremely well-qualified to write the prisoners' story that was about to be read aloud.

Singing to Survive Concert, Chichester, UK, 2013.

CHICHESTER, OCTOBER 2013

The evening was beautifully narrated by Stephanie Cole and Louise Jamieson, two *Tenko* actresses who had a deep understanding of the horrors of camp life. Their words were interwoven with the moving music of the choir. This music, which had inspired and given courage to the prisoners, touched us all very deeply.

Circumstances had somehow brought us all together to remember the camps and the prisoners' hardships. We thought of the wonderful care they had given to each other in the prison camps, the friendship, company, sharing of sparse food and possessions and loving help when sick. Even in times of most extreme suffering or as they died, each person was always surrounded and then remembered by friends.

We thought of ourselves, their descendants, of how our ancestors' lives have affected us and how we may seek to ease their memories and one another's wounds.

William McDougall, the American journalist interned in the men's camps, was so affected by his years in camp that he later became a Catholic priest. McDougall wrote the following in his book, *By Eastern Windows*:

> The first job is to stop hating. But hate does not cease because it is willed to cease. Something else just as solid and powerful has to push out hate and fill the place it occupied. That is the biggest and hardest job – filling the vacancy with positive action. For the replacement must live and breathe for the good of man as does hate for his destruction**.**

Positive Action

Much positive action has taken place since our first trip to the former prison camp sites in 2011. Donations raised by prisoners and their families have been sent to Charitas Hospital in Palembang and to help community projects in Muntok. Families and friends of the prisoners came together at the Chichester vocal orchestra concert, hearing the wonderful music and learning about the suffering but also the resilience of the internees. Historical items have been sent to the Muntok Tinwinning Museum and a separate museum built relating to the camps.

Robert Gray, a descendant of George Gray and his sister-in-law Marjorie Gray, who both died in Muntok, together with the Malayan Volunteers Group, has arranged a plaque in memory of the civilian evacuees for the Changi Museum in Singapore. In 2014, we gathered for the unveiling of the new plaque. It will be seen by tens of thousands of visitors each year, who will learn of 'Singapore's Dunkirk' evacuation and its tragic consequences.

The Bowden family have placed a memorial plaque to Mr Vivian Bowden in the Australian High Commission in Singapore. They have also visited Muntok to bring a plaque that stands outside the old cinema, in the area where Mr Bowden was killed. The people of Muntok built a tiled plinth for this plaque near the village mosque, so it will be respected and well looked after. The Australian Government has created two scholarships for Indonesian students in memory of Mr Vivian Bowden, Australian Official Representative to Singapore.

Despite the dreadful knowledge we have acquired, a measure of happiness has occurred along this journey. Many of us who have visited Palembang and Muntok,

Judy Balcombe and former internee Bob Paterson at Mr Vivian Bowden's Memorial, Muntok.

who attended the Chichester concert or who have been put in contact through the Malayan Volunteers Group are now lifelong friends. These people are like family, perhaps replacing the relatives we lost and the lives we have not known.

We have new friends, too, in Palembang and Muntok – who, although they are not directly connected to the events of the war, have shown a great interest in the prisoners and who have offered us exceptional help and kindness. It is very moving that our Muslim friends have a deep respect for the history and the remains of the largely Christian internees.

The circle of dear friends has expanded and is increasing. It has become like ripples in a pond, ever growing – all of us with a similar heritage and all understanding what one another's grandparents, parents and ourselves have been through.

We thought our work and visits to Bangka Island had ended after placing memorials in Muntok but as general interest grew, we found they were just beginning.

An Internee Returns

In 2014, former internee Neal Hobbs, then aged 89, expressed a wish to visit Palembang and Muntok. We travelled there together with Anthony Pratt, my initial travelling companion in 2011. Revisiting the sites of his captivity must have caused profound emotions for Neal and also Anthony, whose father had been imprisoned with Neal and who had died in Muntok. I am sure Neal recalled his young adult years and the many friends so unnecessarily lost, whom he helped to bury. Neal's cell in Muntok Jail is still labelled 'Room 9'.

In Palembang Jail, where the men had been held for ten months, Neal presented the superintendent with a copy of a drawing of his father and others in a badminton tournament held in the central jail yard. This picture was painted by internee Grixoni, chairman of the Singapore Harbour Board, who later died in Muntok. It is delicately drawn with blue ink on a khaki background, maybe tinted with mud, and the four players are finely sketched, showing their features. The jail superintendent asked Neal what crime he had committed to be placed in prison in 1942 – he was very surprised and answered, 'Nothing, I had done nothing at all. I was 17 years old, here as a prisoner of the Japanese.'

We toured Palembang Jail and donated a large box of toothbrushes, toothpaste, soap, shampoo and other toiletries for the current women prisoners. We entered the dispensary, where prisoners are treated for minor ailments. Neal Hobbs told us the dispensary is in the same room as during

Inside Muntok Jail, Kamar 'Room' 9.

THE EVACUATION OF SINGAPORE

Inside Palembang Jail.

the war but, unlike the barren wartime facility, is now clean and well stocked. Patients who need more complex treatment are taken to the Charitas Hospital. Unlike the limited food available during the war, prisoners now choose from a menu and meals are individually prepared.

Our visit to the jail took place on a Friday, the Muslim Holy Day. We were invited to join the female prisoners in the jail mosque for prayers. The women were very friendly and curious about our presence and made us welcome – another positive memory was created.

The Kindness of Strangers

On our return to Bangka Island, Mr Fakhrizal Abubakar, director of the Timah Tinwinning Museum, arranged for us to visit Jebus (formerly called Djebus), 66km from Muntok. It was here that passengers from my grandfather's lifeboat from the bombed *Giang Bee* had been cared for by Chinese people before being imprisoned. The passengers had included Mrs Gertrude Bean Hinch from the Singapore YWCA, later the leader of the British women in the prison camps.

Also on board had been a 17-year-old girl, Joan Sinclair (later Mrs McIntyre) and her family. Joan later wrote about her 'Girlhood in a Prisoner of War Camp' in the Australian *Women's Weekly Magazine* in November 1969. She described the horrific bombing and sinking of the *Giang Bee* and the overcrowded lifeboat, meant for thirty-four but carrying fifty-six people. On board were elderly men, children, a baby of three months and a badly wounded woman. Passengers had rationed water in a cosmetic jar and sang hymns. After two days and two nights, the lifeboat reached the shore.

On landing, the *Giang Bee* lifeboat passengers had been taken on foot and by boat to Jebus by local people, a journey of six hours. Joan Sinclair writes that two

Jebus River, leading out to sea.

THE EVACUATION OF SINGAPORE

subsequent lifeboats landed at the beach where the *Giang Bee* passengers had spent their first night and that these later arrivals had all been shot and killed. It appears my grandfather had most likely been at Radji Beach and had left for Jebus just before the massacre.

On reaching Jebus, the evacuees were cared for by Chinese families for several days. Joan Sinclair describes how the Chinese people had been very kind, bringing drinking water and also cakes for the children. They provided soap, clothes and protection for the passengers' bare and painful feet. Their luck did not hold, however – after several days in Jebus, Japanese soldiers learned of their presence and took them away to Muntok Jail in trucks.

A Chinese lady, Mrs Sugia Kam who lives in Jebus, growing and selling Heritage Tea, learned of our visit and connection with the town. She later contacted me in Australia to say she had located an elderly Chinese gentleman who had been a child of 5 in Jebus in 1942 and who had met the lifeboat people. Sugia Kam very kindly interviewed Grandpa Malik and sent me photographs, a recording and transcript of the interview.

Grandpa Malik told how an Australian man from the lifeboat had given him a biscuit. He remembered it had tasted good. He told how the Chinese people had given the passengers gunny sacks to wrap around their bare feet, as they had walked through the sharp mangroves.

Joan Sinclair wrote how the only Australian on the truck to Muntok had sworn at the Japanese under his breath. My grandfather was originally Australian. I believe he was the man who had been pulled into the overcrowded *Giang Bee* lifeboat – passenger Murray Miller described this man as having had recent abdominal surgery. My grandfather had a large peptic ulcer operation in Melbourne in November 1941 and had returned to Malaya to recover.

I felt sure my grandfather was the man whom Grandpa Malik had met seventy-seven years ago and whom he remembered. I imagined my grandfather had given the little boy a precious biscuit, although famished himself after two days and nights at sea, thinking of his own two young sons.

I was overwhelmed. I wrote to Sugia Kam and to Grandpa Malik, sending him photos and a packet of Australian biscuits.

Stilt houses, Jebus.

Belalau

To complete our geographic journey, a group of prisoners' families and friends, including the family of British camp leader Mrs Hinch and a former child internee, visited the last prison camp area at Belalau in South-West Sumatra. Like the captives, we travelled by train from Palembang to Lubuk Linggau (formerly Loeboek Linggau), an all-day journey, and then proceeded by road. The prisoners' train windows had been boarded over; we were able to see the jungle and villages we passed as we advanced into the mountains. Any inconveniences we experienced were minor by comparison with their frightful trip, where many died on the journey.

Former women's camp cemetery, Belalau.

Belalau Camp had been an abandoned rubber plantation. The trees were dense, overgrown with jungle and the place completely isolated. For the first time, the prisoners had been very afraid they would never be found and believed this isolation was deliberate. They were placed in derelict huts surrounded by barbed wire. The men's and women's camps were less than a kilometre apart but neither group knew the other was there. A stream served for both drinking and bathing but was soon contaminated. Prisoners ate snails, rats and snakes to supplement their sparse rations. Some crept through the wire fence at night to forage for ubi kayu (tapioca root). If caught, punishment was severe.

Our driver lived at Belalau village, and we were very fortunate to meet the head man, Pak Sepono. He walked with us through the overgrown plantation and jungle to the stream that had run through the men's and women's camps.

We were shown the former women's camp cemetery, where women had carried their friends for burial in the shallow graves they had dug, names burnt onto crosses with a poker. The cemetery is now an empty area behind Pak Sepono's house. He told us that Dutch people sometimes visit to remember their families. There were flowers and butterflies and an air of quiet beauty.

Margaret Dryburgh wrote about the women's camp burial ground in the following poem. She died and was buried here.

THE EVACUATION OF SINGAPORE

> How silent is this place
> The brilliant sunshine filters through the trees,
> The leaves are rustled by a gentle breeze
> A wild and open space
> By shrubs pink tipped, mauve blossomed is o'grown,
> A hush enfolds me, deep as I've known
> Unbroken, save by distant insects' drone
> A jungle clearing, A track through which we bear our load to Him
> How silent is this place, How sacred is this place.

In the middle of the stream, Bob, who had lived in the women's camp from age 2 to 5, found the rock where he had fallen through the bridge and split his head while on an errand for his mother. He recalled the blood dispersing in the water. His hair grew back, but left a permanent white patch.

We followed Pak Sepono through the scarred rubber trees along an overgrown path to the road. A double-storeyed European style house had been the residence of the Japanese camp commandant. In a bizarre act, on one occasion, soldiers had ordered the sick and exhausted prisoners to climb a hill to listen to an orchestra in full uniform, playing German band music. The old house stands on an incline, not really a hill, but it would have felt like a mountain to the prisoners as they struggled up the slope to hear the musicians.

On 25 August 1945, ten days after peace was declared, Captain Seiki Kazue had stood on a table to address prisoners in the men's and women's camps and informed them the war was over. William McDougall wrote that the men displayed little emotion, some shaking hands or crying quietly. Briton Andrew Carruthers, swollen and dying of beriberi, said he was crying from happiness and pain. He was able to be visited by his wife from the women's camp but died before leaving Belalau. Millicent (Molly) Watts-Carter and Australian Army Nurse Pearl Mittelheuser also died still in Belalau Camp.

South Africa Paratrooper Gideon Jacobs and his small band of rescuers entered Belalau camps on 6 September. The location of the camps had been concealed by the Japanese for fear of reprisals when the high death rate and shocking condition of the prisoners became known. Confiscated Red Cross food parcels suddenly materialised from Japanese store rooms, and Allied Liberator aeroplanes dropped parcels with bread – untasted for three years – other foodstuffs, newspapers, medicines and cigarettes.

The camps began to be liberated on 16 September. The Australian Army nurses and the sickest women and children were the first to be evacuated, taken to Lahat by train and flown to Singapore. Bob and his mother

Belalau flower.

BELALAU

were nearly left behind – he was too weak to walk and his mother too weak to carry him.

Courier-Mail war correspondent A.E. Dunstan, who assisted with the evacuation from Belalau, wrote:

> Men and women, emaciated to a grotesque gauntness staggered as we helped them up the steps of the railway carriages on matchstick legs which failed to support them … Some had unsightly ulcers on their bodies, others had fever. Malaria, beri-beri, dysentery, colitis, tuberculosis and general weakness were the commonest complaints. Stretcher cases lay on mattresses. Day was breaking when our train drew out, leaving behind a camp where deaths among internees had exceeded 50 per cent.

Remember Always

A few of us will abide in these joyous fields till the passage of days – time's perfect cycle – has cleansed our clotted stains, and left unspoiled a sense of what is heavenly, and of the pure fire of innocent life.

Virgil, *Aeneid*, book 6

Be quiet with your thoughts of me
I am at rest and feel your power
In every thought and every ebb
With every tide and every moon
When you sleep and when you wake

Eira Day, daughter of child internee Harry Dyne

Finally, a Memorial

The Belalau graves that could be found were moved to Java after the war but most of the Muntok civilian graves had been left behind on Bangka Island and are now built over (men) or lying in a mass grave (women). With the permission of the local government and people of Muntok, a plaque was brought to Bangka Island in 2015, bearing the names of the British, Australian and New Zealand civilians who had died during the war and had no named graves. Funds for this plaque had been raised by the 2013 Chichester Singing to Survive Concert, with music from the original Palembang Women's Prison Camp vocal orchestra and were donated by the Malayan Volunteers Group.

The plaques were made in Melbourne, carried to Singapore and then to Palembang, where they were blessed in the Charitas Hospital chapel at a service sung by the nuns.

Prisoners' families and friends then carried the plaques to Muntok by ferry, the route taken so many times by the captives. Father Paulus Kara blessed the plaques again in the Santa Maria Catholic Church, and a service was held at the Catholic cemetery. We sprinkled bougainvillea petals on the grave of the twenty-five women found during the building of the Pertamina petrol station in 1981. The plaque to all civilians still in Muntok was placed on this grave, which has now been restored.

REMEMBER ALWAYS

The petals were brought to Muntok by Sister Skolastika and Sister Akwilina, two Charitas nuns who travelled with us. They had bought the petals at the Palembang cemetery and carried them to Muntok in a basket.

Mr Robbert van de Rijdt, the director of the Netherlands War Graves Foundation in Jakarta, had contacted Margie Caldicott asking if he may accompany us to Palembang and Muntok. We thanked him for thinking of the Dutch internees but were very touched to learn he also wished to pay his respects to the British, Australian and New Zealand dead. Mr van de Rijdt attended the Charitas Hospital Memorial Service, the placing of the plaque to the internees and the opening of the Muntok Peace Museum.

Remembering those who died in Muntok has been very difficult for some family members, one of whom said that the thought of the town had always been one of dread to him. We hope the support we are able to give to one another and the friendship and understanding shown to us by our Indonesian friends will help to ease some of these deep and long-lasting feelings.

Right: Blessing of memorial plaques, Santa Maria Church, Muntok.

Below left: Memorial grave, Muntok Catholic cemetery.

Below right: Plaques to British, Australian and New Zealand civilians who died in Muntok and who remain buried there, now installed in Muntok Catholic cemetery.

Muntok Peace Museum, September 2015

The people of Muntok are very proud of their long history. The Timah Tinwinning Museum has excellent displays of Bangka Island's ancient history and tin mining methods and houses the Vivian Bullwinkel Galleri, with details of the events of February 1942. We were contacted by a member of the Muntok Heritage Community suggesting there was scope for a separate museum focusing on the long years spent in the prison camps.

Friends and families of the internees and the nurses were contacted and committed enthusiastically to this project, gathering donations to build the small Muntok Peace Museum. The fundraising was a labour of love, and people helped in many ways. Individuals sent sums they could afford, sold personal items and held garage sales to raise money. An afternoon tea was held at the Australian Nurses' Memorial Centre in Melbourne, which was established by nurses Vivian Bullwinkel and Betty Jeffrey after the war.

Vivian and Betty had dreamed of such a centre in memory of their colleagues during their years in camp. On returning home, they had travelled around Victoria in a small car, speaking publicly at hospitals and to community groups to raise funds. At one such gathering they had encountered members of the Dominguez family. Mr Dominguez had escorted the group of women and children away from Radji Beach to Muntok town just prior to the massacre. He and Mrs Dominguez had later died in camp. Their family had not known where the two had died until meeting the fundraising nurses.

A radio station had run a campaign for donations towards the memorial centre, the largest ever held. A building was purchased in Melbourne in 1950 to provide education, accommodation and companionship for all nurses, in memory of nurses who had served in war. This successful outcome was our inspiration to see the Peace Museum come to fruition. It would tell the story of the war years and be a tribute to the many who had died in Muntok Camp and whose graves were not moved to Commonwealth War Graves cemeteries but now lie under houses and the petrol station and in the group grave.

I compiled and sold a cookbook with recipes the prisoners had written down to assuage their hunger while they longed for better days. The Malayan Volunteers Group and the British Association for Cemeteries in South Asia helped with

MUNTOK PEACE MUSEUM, SEPTEMBER 2015

generous donations, BACSA writing that the lost Muntok graves represented one of the saddest stories they had known.

The land was donated by Kampong Menjelang, the site of the former women's prison camp. We asked that the building could also be used as a meeting room for women and a place for children to do their homework. Finally, the first sod was turned in the ground next to the Kampong Menjelang primary school and mosque. Each week photos of the building progress arrived by email and within a few months, the work was completed. The museum comprises a large simple room on pillars, in the traditional Indonesian style. Inside, vertical slatted wall dividers and glass cabinets allow for many displays.

Muntok Memorial Peace Museum.

Families and friends of the internees and nurses sent drawings, photographs, newspaper articles and articles relating to the camps. There is also an Australian Army nurse's uniform from the period.

The museum is a work in progress, and new items will always be welcome.

Peace Museum opening, 2015

The Vice Regent of Muntok officiated at the opening of the Muntok Peace Museum. We were surprised and very touched when he suddenly began to sing in English some words from John Lennon's *Imagine*.

As we stood together under a shaded canopy and listened to the words of this most inspiring song, we truly felt we had indeed found a brotherhood of people who shared and cared about our common history and for the well being of the world. The internees had had no possessions, and they had been hungry beyond belief, but their families' dreams had finally been heard and the prisoners were now all finally remembered.

Visitors to the museum can learn details of the war years in Muntok and the internees' suffering but also about great resilience. We named the museum the Peace Museum in the hope that visitors will learn the importance of peace.

Professor Gary Topping, Catholic archivist in Utah, USA, and biographer of internee American Journalist William McDougall, who became a priest and monsignor after the war, has written that it gladdens his heart to learn that Muntok is no longer only a place of dread but has become a place of beauty and education.

Inside the museum we see copies of drawings of camp life by William Bourke of the New Zealand Navy, who was a prisoner initially in Muntok and then in

THE EVACUATION OF SINGAPORE

the Palembang military camps. His son, Bill Bourke, gave permission for these drawings to be used in the Peace Museum and in this book to demonstrate the prisoners' hardships. In these detailed paintings, we see men running to catch rats to cook for dinner and squatting in a crowded compound over smoking cooking fires. Another of his pictures, stretching over two pages, shows a line of gaunt, ragged men carrying small bundles, staggering as they are moved to yet another prison camp.

There is a painting of the *Tanjong Pinang*, which rescued many people from the *Kuala* and other bombed boats near Pom Pong Island, only to be herself bombed and sunk with further great loss of life. British Nurse Margot Turner, later Brigadier Dame Margot Turner, was one of the few people from this double catastrophe to reach Bangka Island, the only survivor on her raft. She had recalled how, one by one, the victims with her, including children, became dehydrated and died and how she had rolled their bodies into the sea.

Families have sent photos of their relatives with brief biographies. Anthony Pratt gave copies of letters written to his mother by friends who had known his father in the camps, and these are displayed on a lectern. Poignantly, they speak of Donald Pratt's humour and good nature and describe his performances in the camp concerts in Palembang Jail. The letters also tell of Donald Pratt's physical decline after labouring at Pladjoe and his early death, aged 34.

The prison camp diary of Gordon Reis has been copied and enlarged in three volumes and given to the Muntok Peace Museum by Reis' grandson, David Man. This diary tells of Gordon Reis' 'slow death by starvation' and is a detailed account of his deterioration. Reis carefully describes his symptoms and records his decreasing weight until he can write no more.

We see the resourcefulness of the prisoners in the sketch of Mary Brown, wife of Singapore St Andrew's Cathedral choirmaster, wearing the dress she made from Reverend Vic Wardle's striped pyjamas and a sunhat created from a broken umbrella. She has an oversized pair of men's shoes left behind in the Muntok coolie lines by a sailor. In her hands is the coffee grinder borrowed from Dutch internees to grind rice into flour.

Internee Margaret Dryburgh made many fine drawings in the camps. Some she gave as gifts to fellow prisoners for birthdays or simply 'to lift them when they were down'. She drew detailed pictures of the primitive huts and the attempts at a vegetable garden in Palembang barracks camp, never harvested, as the prisoners were moved on before the garden flourished. We also see the rough communal kitchen at Palembang, where huge rice pots burnt the cooks as the boiling rice splashed, a 'bedroom' and the rudimentary Muntok 'hospital' hut. The drawings are an invaluable record of the hardships of prison camp life.

A display in English and Indonesian describes the Palembang Women's Prison camp vocal orchestra and the hope it gave to the choir and the listeners. Also translated into Bahasa Indonesia is Margaret Dryburgh's poem describing the clearing under the trees at Belalau where the women walked to bury their friends.

MUNTOK PEACE MUSEUM, SEPTEMBER 2015

Above left: An apron made as a gift for Margaret Dryburgh from scraps cut from the women's dresses.

Above right: Muntok Peace Museum opening, 2015.

> How silent is this place …
> How sacred is this place.

A thousand folded paper cranes have been placed on the wall of the museum, symbolizing the wish for world peace. There is also a Japanese *obi* 'sash' embroidered with the flying cranes of peace and freedom. We and the local people would like visitors to know that war is very harmful and to try to prevent it from happening again.

The Muntok Peace Museum has an excellent website for people not able to make the physical journey or who wish to look in regularly. It tells the story of the camps, with a biography planned for each person. The website has been created and is added to regularly by David Man, a librarian from Yale and the grandson of internee Gordon Reis, who died in Muntok Jail in 1944. Many people with families in the prison camps have found the website and contacted us for information. The website address is http://muntokpeacemuseum.org

Above left: Australian Army nurse's uniform, Muntok Peace Museum.

Above right: Flying cranes *obi* and 1,000 folded paper cranes, Muntok Peace Museum.

75th Anniversary Gathering, Radji Beach, Muntok

Many groups and individuals have now made the journey to Palembang, Muntok and Belalau since Anthony Pratt, Mr Fakhrizal and I stood alone at the nurses' memorial at Tanjong Kelian lighthouse on Anzac Day 2011. Families and friends of the Australian Army nurses and shipwreck victims, elderly prisoners and representatives from the Australian, British and New Zealand Embassies now visit Bangka Island regularly.

On 16 February 2017, the 75th anniversary of the Bangka Island massacre, a large gathering was held in Muntok. On this day in 1942, the twenty-one Australian Army nurses, civilian women, wounded stretcher cases and servicemen were killed by Japanese soldiers at the place now known as Radji Beach, near Muntok. Nurse Vivian Bullwinkel, British Sailor Ernest Lloyd and American brewer Eric Germann were all wounded in this attack but survived and were able to describe these terrible events to Allied authorities.

The Australian Army nurses who were killed on Radji Beach had served in Singapore and Malaya, caring for wounded servicemen until ordered by the Army to leave Singapore on the SS *Vyner Brooke* on Friday, 13 February 1942. Heartbroken at leaving their patients, they had reluctantly followed military orders. The first group of nurses left on the *Empire Star*, which, although bombed, reached Australia. The *Vyner Brooke*, together with more than 100 vessels, was bombed and sunk by Japanese planes and warships off the shores of Bangka Island. It is estimated that between 4,000 to 5,000 people on these boats were killed in the bombing or drowned.

Many had floated or swum in the sea for up to three days before reaching land. At Radji Beach near Muntok, Japanese soldiers had first ordered servicemen and civilian men around a headland where they were shot and bayonetted. The Australian Army nurses caring for wounded stretcher cases on the beach and one civilian woman were marched into the sea and machine-gunned. Stretcher cases were then killed with bayonets and rifle butts. All the nurses were killed except Vivian Bullwinkel, who was shot in her side but survived.

On 16 February 2017, family members of five of these nurses gathered in Muntok to attend memorial services. They were joined by the Australian Ambassador to Indonesia, Australian and British defence attachés, current Australian Army nurses,

75TH ANNIVERSARY GATHERING, RADJI BEACH, MUNTOK

Australian and British Army chaplains and families of civilians who died in the Muntok prison camps. The granddaughters of British Sailor Stoker Ernest Lloyd, who had been shot through the scalp on Radji Beach but had survived, made the long journey from England to attend. Many Indonesian officials, doctors and nurses also attended the services.

In the early morning, a formal service for the Australian Army nurses and others killed on Radji Beach was held in the Timah Tinwinning Building Museum. Following the eulogy and prayers, a bell was tolled for each murdered nurse.

Wreaths were laid by nurses' families, the Australian and British governments, the Government of Banka Barat (West Bangka Island) and the Malayan Volunteers Group. The MVG wreath was made from knitted and crocheted red poppies made by internees' and nurses' families.

We then visited the nurses' memorial at the Tanjong Kelian lighthouse for additional laying of wreaths. Because the nurses were military personnel, this site is maintained by the Australian Office of War Graves. A rusted shipwreck lies close to the shore; a visual reminder of the many boats sunk nearby in February 1942.

A service in memory of the civilian men, women and children who were imprisoned and died in the Muntok camps was then held at Kampong Menjelang, the former women's prison camp site. Wreaths were laid by the Australian and British defence attachés and by families. David Man and I read the names of the ninety civilians who had died in this camp, including both our grandfathers, and who remain buried there in 'the lost graves of Muntok'. David and I scattered bougainvillea petals, the custom at Indonesian funerals.

In the afternoon, the large group gathered on Radji Beach for an address by Michael Noyce, the nephew of murdered Australian Army Nurse Kathleen Neuss. He described the events of 16 February 1942, indicating the likely landmarks of the massacre. Australian and British army chaplains led prayers – including for the many killed on Radji Beach whose names will never be known.

The families of massacred nurses Matron Irene Drummond, Kathleen Neuss, Dorothy (Bud) Elmes, Elaine Balfour-Ogilvy and Clarice Halligan waded into the water to place wreaths on the waves. 'Chin up, girl. I'm proud of you and I love you all,' Matron Irene Drummond had called to her nurses as she walked with them into the sea to be shot.

We were moved beyond belief as a line of serving Australian Army nurses in full, immaculate uniform spontaneously held hands and walked into the water, as their fallen colleagues had done seventy-five years before. We were further very touched when a group of local Indonesian nurses and doctors in their spotless white uniforms held a memorial service on the sand and threw petals into the water in memory of the nurses and all other victims.

Investigations are ongoing as to whether the nurses were assaulted before being killed. There is evidence that this is likely to have occurred. Additional information will be published soon by other researchers.

The fate of the bodies of those killed on Radji Beach is unknown. They had been seen by Robert Seddon, who also observed the massacre while swimming out at sea, by massacre survivors Eric Germann and Ernest Lloyd and soldiers in coming days. It is likely their remains were washed out to sea or less likely that they were buried by Japanese soldiers to conceal them, by Allied soldiers or by local people. Their resting place is not known, but they are remembered by their families and friends and now by their governments.

A memorial plaque has been made and installed on the headland around which the men were killed. Tidal studies show that this was the likely area where the nurses' bodies would have been carried back into shore. A sentence in Indonesian informs the reader that this coastline is hallowed ground.

Muntok Red Cross and Other Volunteers

We are very fortunate to have the strong friendship of the local people in Muntok and are most grateful for their interest and care. The Muntok Red Cross and other volunteers laboured for many months preparing for our visit, grading the rough dirt road through a plantation to the area near Radji Beach, formerly only accessible by sea or on foot, and clearing the foreshore and areas around memorials.

They also worked tirelessly to assist with flood relief. In the weeks before our visit in 2017, extreme floods had damaged many houses on Bangka Island and the bridge on the only road linking the port of Muntok to the airport and capital in Pangkalpinang was washed away. Volunteers helped to repair homes and erected a temporary bridge so supplies could reach other towns; this also enabled us to reach Muntok safely. Convoys of vehicles driven by volunteers transported us on the six-hour round trip from Pangkalpinang when the ferry from Palembang was cancelled. Our group took up a collection so the volunteers could continue their flood relief work, and we now help to support Covid and other humanitarian work of the Muntok Red Cross.

A cultural evening was held for us in Muntok, with ceremonial dances. We were presented with a beautifully illustrated book about the women's camp written in English and Indonesian, with drawings by a local artist. A poem had been especially written for the occasion. This describes the emotions of Vivian Bullwinkel when she remembers her slain colleagues:

> Remember although you died from the world, You are alive in my mind …
> Rest in peace, my friends
> And take my hand to join me in Heaven.

The people of Muntok have a strong understanding of and respect for their history, a part of which is our history. Future visitors will learn a great deal about the past and will be made most genuinely welcome.

Walk for Humanity, Radji Beach, February 2018

In February 2018, a smaller but no less passionate group gathered in Muntok. Two members of the Australian Embassy in Jakarta were present, together with the families of Radji Beach nurses Matron Irene Drummond, Kathleen Neuss, Dorothy (Bud) Elmes; the president of the Australian Nurses' Memorial Centre in Melbourne, Mrs Arlene Bennett; and former Naval Defence Attaché to Singapore Lieutenant Commander Bruce Bird, while I represented the civilian shipwreck victims and internees.

A red carpet and ceremonial dance greeted our arrival at the Yasmin Hotel, showing how deeply the local people respect the Second World War victims. On 16 February, we assembled at the former women's prison camp site at Kampong Menjelang, where I read the names of the eighty-eight British, Australian and New Zealand internees who had died in the camps and who are believed to remain buried in Muntok.

The Australian Defence Attaché to Indonesia read in both English and Indonesian the moving poem by missionary internee Margaret Dryburgh, reminding people that to us Kampong Menjelang is a place of reverence. In the face of horror and death, the women prisoners had carried their friends to bury them in hand-dug graves under the rubber trees. Margaret Dryburgh and her fellow prisoners drew strength from the peace and beauty of their surroundings:

> … A jungle clearing
> A track through which we bear our load to Him
> How silent is this place
> How sacred is this place

To end this service, I read words from a poem by internee Marjory Jennings who, like Margaret Dryburgh, had died at Belalau, the last prison camp. Marjory wrote many poems in camp in the pages of her Bible, which is now in the Imperial War Museum in London. Marjory Jennings had a vision of a peace after the war:

THE EVACUATION OF SINGAPORE

> Secluded here one might believe
> All in the world was peaceful too
> Until the shattered folk appear
> And sentries spoil the lovely view.
>
> One day all this must end, and we
> Who live to see succeeding years
> Must in the new world strive to build
> A lasting peace, from blood and tears.

From Kampong Menjelang, we drove to the nurses' memorial near the lighthouse at Tanjong Kelian. This lighthouse was one of two seen by the shipwrecked victims and had served as a beacon for people in lifeboats, on rafts or in the water, struggling to reach the shore. A local eyewitness told how the Japanese had moved the lighthouse beam so that Allied boats could be found and bombed.

A large plaque on the nurses' memorial bears the names of all sixty-five Australian Army Bangka Island nurses – the twelve who drowned in the bombing of the SS *Vyner Brooke*, the twenty-one massacred on the beach, the four who died in Muntok and the four who died in Belalau, as well as the twenty-four nurses who survived the war, struggling to care for sick women and children in camp. Wreaths and flowers were laid in memory of all the nurses, civilian and military massacre victims and all those killed at sea. A photo of Stoker Ernest Lloyd, who had first survived the bombing of the *Prince of Wales* in Singapore, then the sinking of the *Vyner Brooke* and had been shot but lived through the Radji Beach massacre, was presented at the nurses' memorial and later hung in the Peace Museum. His granddaughters had told us whenever they grumbled as little children, their grandfather would remark that: 'Worse things happen at sea!'

In the afternoon, we were taken to the elevated site overlooking the Bangka Strait. The mainland of Sumatra can be seen faintly across the water, so near and yet so very far. In this stretch of sea, the multitude of boats leaving Singapore had been bombed and sunk by the Japanese air and naval fleets en route to Palembang, with enormous loss of life. The massacre of nurses, civilians and servicemen had occurred on the beach below.

We climbed colourful tiled steps to the new memorial plaque in memory of all who lost their lives in this region. The location was chosen because the ocean where so many lost their lives, the cove where the men were taken to be killed and Radji Beach itself can all be seen clearly. Speeches were delivered by Michael Noyce, nephew of Nurse Kathleen Neuss; by Georgina Banks, great-niece of nurse Dorothy Elmes; and by Lieutenant Commander Mark Graichen of the Australian Navy. Muntok's Catholic priest, Father Paulus Kara, blessed the memorial and those it represents. The words of Margaret Dryburgh's Captives Hymn was spoken.

Wreaths were laid, including one in memory of Major William Alston Tebbutt, who had been in charge of the Australian Army nurses on the *Vyner*

WALK FOR HUMANITY, RADJI BEACH, FEBRUARY 2018

Above left: Memorial to all victims near Radji Beach, Muntok.

Above right: Inaugural Walk for Humanity, Muntok, 16 February 2018.

Brooke and had attempted to keep track of them while imprisoned in Palembang and Changi.

Replicating the actions of the current serving Australian Army nurses who visited Muntok in 2017 for the 75th anniversary of 1942, we linked arms and walked into the sea, scattering flowers and wreaths. This action has now become the annual Walk for Humanity, which is held on the beach at Muntok each 16 February. Everyone present remembers the Second World War victims and the many who suffer in wars and conflicts today, pledging peace and vowing that violence will not have the last word on Radji Beach.

The Origin and Location of Radji Beach

Today, the massacre of the nurses, civilians and servicemen is said to have occurred at 'Radji Beach', but this name is not on any current or old Indonesian or Dutch map and the origin of the word remains unclear. The first mention of Radji Beach that we can find appears in an Australian newspaper, the *Newcastle Sun*, on Friday, 9 November 1945. Here we read that:

> The Australian flag which flew over the 1st Casualty Clearing Station in Malaya and which was mended by nurses, eight of whom were later massacred by the Japanese on Radji Beach, Banka Island, will be presented to St. Philip's Presbyterian Church and later dedicated by the Rev. A.R. McVittie next Sunday.
>
> The 1st C.C.S. later went to Thailand to work on the Thailand-Burma railway. A memorial service will be held at St. Philip's at 7.15 on Sunday night in memory of Australian nursing sisters who lost their lives during the war.

When Vivian Bullwinkel revisited Muntok in the 1990s to choose a site for the nurses' memorial, she said she did not know the origin of the name Radji Beach.

Some possibilities for the name are:

1. There is a coral reef near the Tanjong Kelian lighthouse at Muntok called Korang Hadjie, pronounced for us by an Indonesian friend as 'Korang Ar-jee'.
2. Hadjie or Radjie can be used to describe a senior Muslim man in a village. Vivian Bullwinkel would have met such a person when requesting help from villagers at Kampong Genggilang or Old Menjelang after the massacre.
3. Radjie is a word in Scottish dialect meaning a violent tantrum. Could this have been as a code word by Northern English or Scottish women in the camps to describe the massacre? The massacre was never discussed openly to protect Vivian Bullwinkel. Margaret Dryburgh and Dr Margaret Thomson were Scots.

THE ORIGIN AND LOCATION OF RADJI BEACH

4. Rajik is a Hindu word for 'shining' or 'diamond' – there are alluvial diamonds in Indonesia, sometimes found on the sea shore. This word could also perhaps have referred to the diamond ring given to father-in-law of 'the Mother with the Ring'.
5. Toraji is a tropical flower found in the area (Campanula).
6. A word maybe transcribed by mistake by Allied authorities after the war.
7. Lastly, an Indonesian dictionary tells us that the old root word 'Raja' is associated with violence such as stabbing, physical punishment, torture or murder. 'Rajeh' means 'in shreds, broken or torn to pieces'. It is possible that local villagers spoke in whispers about the massacre site using such a word and that it was recorded by Dutch and Australian army investigators after the war, believing it to be a proper name.

I have studied old and contemporary map and there is no beach at or near Muntok with this name. The origin of the word Radji is still unclear. Any thoughts or information will be gratefully received.

Because the name of Radji Beach is not known to Indonesian people today, the exact location of the massacre is unconfirmed. Local historians believe the nurses and stretcher cases were killed on the beach named Teluk Menggeris or Mangaris (called after a large local tree) and that the men were taken around the point of Tanjong Sabajau to be killed. A document from the Australian National Archives has a map drawn by Sergeant Yemm, a war crimes investigator, showing the region of the massacre as described to him in 1945 as having occurred at Teluk Menggeris.

Teluk Menggeris has long been known in Muntok also as Teluk Inggris or English Bay, where local people believe the English (European) nurses and civilians were murdered, with the men being killed nearby. Vivian Bullwinkel described finding two streams with fresh water as she hid in the jungle, and maps of the area show such streams in this location. Local maps from 1942 show footpaths leading from Teluk Menggeris Beach to the nearby Kampongs of Gelinggang and Old Menjelang. More research is taking place to help locate the exact sites of the tragedy. Muntok Historian Mr Fakhrizal Abubakar and his staff from the Timah Tinwinning Museum have walked for several hours through the jungle from the Old Menjelang area to Teluk Menggeris trying to locate the now-overgrown original path and have interviewed elderly residents.

In Kampong Menjelang, we visited the 'Mother with the Ring' and her family. This older lady has two treasured possessions – the small diamond ring given to her father-in-law by a lady with two children, either shipwreck victims leaving the beach or prisoners in the camp, in return for food. The mother also has a pocket watch from Robinsons department store in Singapore, given to her father-in-law by a passenger from the boats or a prisoner. The family kept these items carefully hidden from the Japanese; they are now looked after safely and brought out to show visitors.

THE EVACUATION OF SINGAPORE

Ring given to local man in exchange for food, now cared for by 'the Mother'.

During the war, the mother's father-in-law had lived in 'Old Menjelang', a previous village near former Kampong Genggilang. These small fishing villages were near the area now called Radji Beach but no longer exist and no trace can be seen. It is likely that the party of women and children walking from Radji Beach to Muntok, led by Mr Dominguez, passed near Old Menjelang and Kampong Genggilang as they walked to Muntok town and requested help from the villagers there. Village women gave Vivian Bullwinkel food for herself and Private Kinsley as they hid in the jungle for twelve days after the massacre. The villagers were aware of the killings on the beach. They also knew that Muntok had experienced aerial bombing by the Japanese, that the town had been captured and Indonesian women assaulted. Fearing for their lives, the people of Old Menjelang and Kampong Genggilang deserted their homes and never returned.

The current memorial plaque to the Australian Army nurses, all victims killed on the beach and all who died in the water, has been placed one beach further north of the massacre site at Tanjong Betumpak. This is accessible by a bumpy four-wheel drive, whereas Teluk Menggeris must be reached by motorboat, motorbike or by a long walk through the jungle. This memorial, on a small headland, overlooks Teluk Menggeris, Tanjong Sabajau and the large graveyard of the Bangka Strait. In this calm and clear water, up to 5,000 people on more than one hundred boats fleeing Singapore lost their lives. Human bones continued to be found washed up for many years.

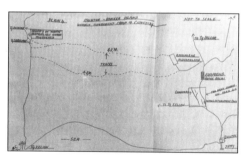

Above left: Map drawn by Sergeant Yemm, part of the post-war investigating team while in Muntok 1945, showing the area where local people told him the nurses and men were killed. (Australian National Archives)

Above right: Aerial view of massacre region (reverse view, looking back to Muntok), courtesy Mr Fakhrizal Abubakar, Director of Timah Tinwinning Museum, Muntok.

THE ORIGIN AND LOCATION OF RADJI BEACH

The area of the massacre. The men are believed to have been killed around the bottom point of Tanjong (Cape) Sabadjau, then the nurses and stretcher cases between Tanjong Sabadjau and Tanjong Besajap at Teluk Menggeris, also called Teluk Inggris (after 'English' people killed here). This area is a few kilometres north-west of Muntok.

Above left: Teluk Menggeris, also known as Teluk Inggris (English Bay).

Above middle: Teluk Sabadjau.

Above right: Mr Idris.

We left Muntok remembering the victims of the massacre and all who suffered during the war. We resolved to seek more information, to perpetuate the memory of those who suffered in the war, to share our knowledge among prisoners' families and to help the people of Muntok today.

Providing a nurse's scholarship in Muntok, involvement in a local women's and children's clinic, assisting the current prisoners in Muntok Jail and helping to teach English are planned projects for the future. Since 2020, as Friends of Bangka Island, our group has supported the Muntok Red Cross in its Covid-19 work and, during the pandemic, has fundraised to purchase medical equipment and a Covid ambulance for the Red Cross. By chance, the ambulance was delivered on 25 April 2021, which is Anzac Day.

A Muntok Resident's Memories of the Massacre on the Beach

Fakhrizal Abubakar, director of Timah Tinwinning Museum, interviewed Idris bin Suhud on 10 March 2018 about old Kampong Menjelang and the massacre on the beach. This is his report of that conversation:

Mr Idris bin Suhud was born in 1934 and is 84 years old now (2018). He is a second child from a family of five children. Mr Idris was born and lived in Old Kampong Menjelang, located near Kampong Gelinggang. In 1942 Mr Idris was aged 8.

THE EVACUATION OF SINGAPORE

Mr Idris said that when the Japanese came to attack Muntok, he heard the sound of bombing in two areas, first in Muntok and then the sea around 'Betumpak Headland'.

According to Mr Idris, when the massacre happened on the beach, the people of the village did not know about it at first. A few days after this incident, villagers wanted to go fishing and saw that there were many corpses on the beach and told other villagers. But not many wanted to look, for fear of the Japanese soldiers. The villagers did not dare to bury the bodies. Only a few corpses were buried, which were located in their hut. They were very afraid.

The corpses were carried by ocean currents and eventually drifted away. After a few days, they could not be seen.

People in Old Kampong Menjelang worked as gardeners in the area near the beach. Mr Idris said his parents told him there were one or two 'white people' who survived, and lived in their garden hut near the beach, not in the kampong. They did not allow the foreigners to live in the kampong for fear of the Japanese. The people ate some food from the village at the garden hut. Then one or two brave residents took the white people and showed them the path to Muntok.

Mr Idris said that for weeks and months after the Second World War tragedy, many skulls of victims were found around 'Tanjung Berani' beach, sometimes up to twenty skulls. Many skulls and bones also spread along the beach from 'Tanjung Batu Berani' to 'Menjelang' beach. Idris saw these skulls himself.

According to the old people in the village, Mr Idris said the bombing tragedy was located in 'Karang Rawan' area and the shooting tragedy located in between the 'Batu Betumpak' and 'Teluk Menggeris' areas. As a child, Mr Idris also saw the Japanese warships from people's gardens by climbing the trees near the 'Tanah Merah' beach.

Mr Idris said that when the Japanese came, many foreigners walked into Old Kampong Menjelang, which was a meeting point. People feared the Japanese, so they hid from them.

Mr Idris said, a few years later, there were a lot of women and children in the 'Bedeng' area (the Japanese camp), which is now a sports field, near the Kampong Keranggan Atas. Mr Idris also saw foreign women walking in the little road near 'Bedeng' carrying buckets of faeces to throw into the forest. This was near the edge of Muntok town.

Mr Idris said that after 1942, Gelinggang village was abandoned for fear of the Japanese and only durian trees and cempedak trees grew there.

Above: From investigators' report 1946, Australian National Archives.

Left: Fakhrizal Abubakar, Mr Idris and friend.

An End to War and a True Peace

> Belief in final peace is our only hope and redemption.
> Internee Gordon Reis

A Tree for World Peace, February 2020

In 2020, families of the Australian Army nurses killed on Radji Beach approached the Japanese Embassy in Australia, inviting a representative to attend the Bangka Island Memorial Service on 16 February. The invitation was forwarded to the Japanese Embassy in Jakarta and Mr Takonai Susumu, the political advisor to the Japanese Embassy in Indonesia, travelled to Muntok. He joined with Gary Quinlan, the Australian ambassador to Indonesia, and his staff, the Australian, British and New Zealand defence attachés, families and friends of the Australian Army nurses and civilians and Muntok officials and local people, as all held hands in the Walk for Humanity on Radji Beach.

To mark the occasion, a rose bush was purchased and embassy officials from all four countries joined in planting the Tree for World Peace. Mr Robbert van der Rijdt, director of the Netherlands War Graves Foundation in Indonesia, sent apologies on behalf of the Dutch prisoners as he was preparing for the visit of the Dutch king coming to remember Dutch servicemen killed in 1942 in the Battle of the Sunda Strait.

Above left: New Zealand Defence Attaché, Gary Quinlan, Australian Ambassador to Indonesia, British and Australian Defence Attachés and John Bullwinkel, nephew of Australian Army Nurse Vivian Bullwinkel.

Above right: Walk for Humanity, Muntok, 16 February 2020.

THE EVACUATION OF SINGAPORE

The Tree for Peace was placed in the garden of the Sudirman Homestay opposite the Timah Tinwinning Museum and Muntok Jail. Mrs Abdurrachim and her family made us very welcome, and we were all given a beautiful glass flower as a memento of the occasion. Here this special rose bush is lovingly nurtured, and we are and we are told, is blooming beautifully. A Peace Park has now been created in this garden.

Scattered petals.

Planting the Tree for Peace.

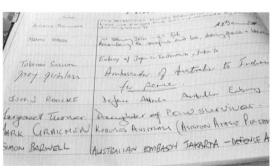

Visitors' book, Muntok Peace Museum, 16 February 2020.

Pimikir, Reflections

People suffered vastly in the Second World War, as in all wars, but in these pages, I have tried to tell how something positive is taking place despite the terrible events of the past.

Muntok lies on the western tip of Bangka Island, Indonesia, overlooking the Bangka Strait and Sumatra. The name Muntok means 'the end of the road', as it is the last town before reaching the sea. This location *was* the end of the road for the many people who suffered and died there between 1942 and 1945.

These events occurred over eighty years ago, but the tragedy has not been forgotten. A memorial to the sixty-five army nurses from the SS *Vyner Brooke* stands near the Tanjong Kelian lighthouse at Muntok. A plaque in memory of all those killed at Radji Beach on 16 February 1942 and in the sinking of over one hundred ships has been installed on the headland overlooking the Bangka Strait. Memorial plaques have been taken to the site of the former men's prison camp in Muntok Jail, to Kampong Menjelang where the women were imprisoned, to the Timah Tinwinning Museum and to the Charitas Hospital in Palembang.

The people whose graves were lost after the war and who now lie in a group grave and under houses and a petrol station have their names recorded on plaques at Muntok's Catholic cemetery. The Muntok Peace Memorial Museum at Kampong Menjelang has been built. Here people can learn about their families, the war years and the importance of peace.

But our focus is not only on remembering past tragedy. We first came to Muntok in 2011 looking for our families' graves. We did not find them but instead, we found our history, new friends and a new family. The Regent of West Bangka addressed the town in during our visit in 2012, explaining that local peoples' ancestors and our ancestors had all lived in Muntok at the same time, meaning we are all part of the same family now.

Psychiatrist Viktor Frankl lost his entire family in Auschwitz in the war. He later taught that it is important for man to search for a meaning in life, whatever tragedy has occurred in the past. And this is what I think has happened here. Our sorrow has been eased by the warmth of our new friendships, remembering the events of the past and in helping to build a better future. The friendships and this work are ever-expanding.

Donations from internees' and nurses' families have helped deepen the original camp well at Kampong Menjelang, which is still in use, and to dig a new well

THE EVACUATION OF SINGAPORE

Singapore Far East Moon.

for the villagers. The 'Singing to Survive' Chichester concert funds assisted the Kampong Menjelang school to buy new computers and to repair the classroom ventilation system.

The Australian Government now gives annual scholarships to Indonesian students in memory of its official representative, Mr Vivian Bowden. There are plans for a nurse from Muntok to study in Australia and for Australian Army nurses to volunteer in Muntok. Australians who visited Muntok are helping secondary and university students with English language conversation online.

The annual Walk for Humanity now occurs near Radji Beach each 16 February. In 2020, the embassies of Australia, Great Britain, New Zealand and Japan planted the Muntok Tree for Peace, now made into a Peace Garden. During the Covid pandemic, online memorial services were held and candles for peace were lit around the world.

Vivian Bullwinkel brought her knowledge of tropical diseases learned in prison camp to become director of nursing at Melbourne's Fairfield Infectious Disease Hospital after the war. Our group is now helping to support the Muntok Red Cross in their essential infectious disease control work during the Covid pandemic and has purchased equipment and a Covid ambulance.

A new rose, Singapore Far East Moon, has been named for the *Vyner Brooke* nurses and is in memory of all Far East prisoners of war and civilian internees. It is yellow to represent friendship, mateship and compassion. Our rose was released in Australia in 2022, eighty years after 1942, so people could plant a beautiful tribute in their gardens. These prisoners began their unexpected journey in Singapore and they and their loved ones at home all looked up at the same bright moon.

The events of the war were a tragedy for so many, leaving indelible stains and must not be forgotten. It is important to remember the victims but also for people to learn that war is a dreadful thing and to do everything possible to prevent it.

Sister Wilma Oram Young, one of the twenty-four Australian Army nurses who survived both the bombing of the SS *Vyner Brooke* and the prison camps, spoke these words addressing a school group in 1971:

> Whatever you think about war and the issues involved today, do not condemn your own dead fathers and grandfathers, do not call our maimed and wounded men and women fools. Remember in sympathy and understanding their motives and sacrifices.
>
> Work with all your might to spread goodwill, understanding and appreciation among all the people of this little, vulnerable and lonely

PIMIKIR, REFLECTIONS

world, irrespective of race, colour and belief, so that never again will young men and women have to sacrifice themselves to preserve their way of life against the threat of those who would destroy it.

Although Muntok was, for many, 'the end of the road', it is hoped that the journey will continue to lead forward. We hope that Muntok may be a place that is no longer only a place of dread to prisoners and their families but one where these unexpected journeys have produced a measure of peace, harmony, caring and goodwill.

Friends of Bangka Island Muntok Red Cross Covid Ambulance.

Poems

Mr Vivian Bowden wrote a poem describing his beloved home in Japan as he left for boarding school in Australia in 1900, reproduced here by permission of his son. As Australia's Official Representative to Singapore, Mr Bowden was killed by guards outside the Muntok Cinema on 17 February 1942, but we have his poem telling of the picturesque land of his childhood that he held in his heart.

Home
There is a land that I call home, far off in old Japan:
The land of lotus blossoms, the maple and the fan;
The land of cryptomeria pines, beneath whose fragrant shade, The old red lacquer temples doze, while generations fade.

A land of lakes and rippling streams, where rainbow colours blend,
Where snow-clad Fuji sits and waits until the world shall end.
Would that I might return once more, ere my life's sands are run:
Land of the Gold Chrysanthemum! Land of the rising Sun!

To hear the old familiar sounds, – the ceaseless temple drum, The clatter, clatter of the clogs as people go and come.
To wander once again about the temple's sacred grounds,
And hear once more the old bronze bell, as fleeted hours it sounds.

But 'tis too late – my day is past: Japan I'll see no more:
I can but dream of what I called my home in days of yore. The mind must now replace the eyes, their visions it must see,
For though I am now far from home, my thoughts lie o'er the sea.

At Christmas 1942, internee William Probyn Allen wrote in a poem to his wife from Palembang Prison Camp:

Have faith, my love, although the night is dark,
the day will break
and Peace and Good will come to men at last.

POEMS

Prisoner Margery Jennings wrote in her Bible that a lasting peace must be built in the new world, and missionary Margaret Dryburgh prayed in the Captives' Hymn:

> May the day of freedom dawn,
> Peace and Justice be reborn.

They wrote of beauty, their memories, their dreams and hopes for the future. We have their words and their stories to inspire and to guide us.

Rosebush for peace, Muntok.

Selamat Tinggal – Goodbye and Peace Be With You

If you remember, this story began in Western Australia in 1882 with a train ride, a lost hat and a query at a railway station. A man strayed from his wife, then fled from the consequences to seek his life in another land. This relocation meant that his son, my grandfather, was later caught in the events of a terrible war.

My grandfather and many others had crowded on board a fleet of small, brave boats trying to escape Singapore for safety. This sudden, unexpected journey led them into the path of Japanese planes and warships, where their ships were bombed and sunk and thousands lost their lives. Twenty-one Australian Army nurses, civilians and servicemen were executed on the beach near Muntok, now known as Radji Beach. Australia's representative, Vivian Bowden, was executed defending a British soldier. Many others were killed in the area, although their names and the details may never be known.

The civilian internees and prisoners of war of the Japanese suffered greatly during three and a half years of cruelty and gross neglect. They were moved backwards and forwards between increasingly dreadful prison camps, where one half of men and one third of women died from disease and starvation. Their journeys lived on in survivors' minds and in those of all the families.

This is a true story that happened to real people. By effort and good fortune, we can try to write a sequel where we can remember our families and their suffering but form new friendships and try to make a difference to other people's lives. We can help people to learn from history, to be aware and to try to live peacefully. It is not possible to change the past, but we can try to heal it, our families and ourselves through this bond with our Indonesian friends.

Very importantly, we hope that visitors to the Muntok Peace Museum, the Peace Museum website, or the Muntok Peace Garden, or all who become aware of this story in other ways will understand the full circle these unexpected journeys and pathways to peace has taken and will strive for peace in their lives and in the world.

http://muntokpeacemuseum.org

Terima Kasih (Thank You)

These details have been written in memory of our families and their friends who suffered indescribable hardship during the Second World War. They are also a tribute to their descendants.

I would like to thank our wonderful friends in Muntok and Palembang who have helped us so much during our visits and who are helping to keep the memory of the prisoners alive. In the words of the Regent of West Bangka Island, 'We are all part of the same family now.'

I would also like to thank our friends and colleagues who have helped us find and remember the 'lost graves of Muntok', to establish and maintain the Muntok Peace Museum and to record this history: Mrs Rosemary Fell, Jonathan Moffatt and Michael Pether of the Malayan Volunteers Group, Mr Muhammad Rizki, Mr Fakhrizal Abubakar, Margie Caldicott, David Man, Anthony Pratt, Lieutenant Commander Bruce Bird, Arlene Bennett, Lavinia Warner, John Misto and many others.

We will never forget our dear friend the late Roderick Suddaby, keeper of documents at the Imperial War Museum, London, who inspired us in this search he called 'our work' and which, when very ill, he asked us to continue.

> And some there be who are perished as though they had never been.
> Their bodies are buried in peace but their names liveth for evermore.
> The children will tell of their wisdom. (Ecclesiasticus, Chapter 44)

Saya Akhirnya Mengerti – Now I Understand.

Acknowledgements

Many thanks are also due to those who assisted in my research, permitted material to be used in this book and allowed their stories to be told. I would like to sincerely thank the following people and organisations and apologise profoundly for any omissions.

Pak Abisofyan, writing of Mr William Probyn Allen, Mr Afan, Ralph Armstrong, Australian Embassy to Indonesia, Australian Nurses Memorial Centre, Singapore National Library, Graham Blick, diary of Shelagh Brown, family of Carrie (Jean) Ashton, Georgina Banks, Boswell family, Bill Bourke, family of Mr Vivian Bowden, Ron Bridge, British Association for Cemeteries in South Asia, memoirs of Jock Brodie, Broken Hill Library, family of Gordon Burt, Catholic Archives, Utah, Dr Christine Carberry-Hanson, Charitas Hospital, Palembang, Raimy Che Ross and Dr Colin Goodwin for their kind translations, family of Helen Colijn, Barbara Coombes, Eira Day for her poems, Philip Dickson, family of Kenneth Dohoo, family of Margaret Dryburgh, Far East Prisoners of War Family, Friends of Bangka Island, Judy Fowler, family of Oswald W Gilmour, Robert Gray, family of Ellen (Mavis) Hannah, family of Hal Hammett, Mr and Mrs Herman, Syarifudin Isa, family of Betty Jeffrey, family of Margery Jennings, Mrs Sugia Kam, Father Paulus Kara and Muntok Catholic Cemetery, diary of Horace Kendall, family of Dr Lentze, family of Ernest Lloyd, Malayan Volunteers Group, Grandpa Malik, family of Leslie McCann, family of Dr Albert Stanley McKern, diary of Murray James Vijfhuis Miller, writings of William McDougall, Mother with the Ring, Muntok Heritage Community, Muntok Nurses and Internees Group, Muntok Red Cross, Netherlands War Graves Foundation, Jenny Novick, Michael Noyce, Bob Paterson, P.T. Timah, diary of Gordon Reis, memoirs of Duncan Robertson, Theo Rottier, Mr Idris bin Sahud, Janey Shephard, writings of Joan Sinclair, Pattie Smith, Chris Stapleton, writing of Wilma Oram Young, Mrs Sudirman and Feni, Mr Takonai Susumu, Ronnie Taylor, Dr Yuki Tanaka, Staff of Timah Tinwinning Museum, Professor Gary Topping, memoirs of Harry Walker, Paddy Walker-Taylor, Isidore Warman, Joan Wilson, Desmond and Gillian Woodford, Mr Robbert van de Rijdt, Ni Komang Suriati, Jane Booker Nielsen, my very patient family and friends and others.

Bibliography

Books and papers about the evacuation of Singapore and its consequences, the Australian Army nurses and the Muntok, Palembang and Belalau internees.

A Woman's War, the exceptional life of Wilma Oram, Barbara Angell
Australia's Forgotten Prisoners, Civilians interned by the Japanese in World War 2, Christina Twomey
Blanchie, Alstonville's Inspirational World War 2 Nurse, Ian Kirkland
British Civilians and the Japanese War in Malaya and Singapore 1942–1945, Joseph Kennedy
Bullwinkel, Norman G. Manners
By Eastern Windows, If I Get out Alive and *Six Bells off Java*, William H. McDougall
Camp News, edited by W.P. Allen and William McDougall, illustrated by Th. J.A. Romkes-Agerbeek, courtesy Professor G. Topping, Catholic Archivist, Salt Lake City, Utah
Captives, Australian Army Nurses in Japanese Prison Camps, Catherine Kenny
Facing the Bow, European Women in Colonial Malaya 1919–1945, Jean Teasdale
Family Journal – the War Years, Betty M. Wardle
Hidden Horrors, Japanese War Crimes in World War 2, Dr Yuki Tanaka
I Will Sing to the End, Ian McLeod (son of Dorothy McLeod)
Malayan and Singapore newspapers, Singapore National Library Board
Malayan Climax, Carline Reid
Matron A.M. Sage, *A Tribute by Betty Jeffrey*, Australian Army Nurses
No Bamboo for Coffins, David Elio Roberts
On Radji Beach, Ian W. Shaw
Pigeon's Luck, Vladimir Tretchikoff
Portrait of a Nurse, Pat Darling (nee Gunther)
Prelude to the Monsoon, G.F. Jacobs
Remembering Tenko, Andy Priestner
Short Cruise on the Vyner Brooke, Ralph E.H. Armstrong
Singapore's Dunkirk, Geoffrey Brooke
Singapore to Freedom, Oswald W. Gilmour
Soldier Surgeon in Malaya, Thomas Hamilton
Song of Survival, Helen Colijn
Spotlight on Singapore, Denis Russell-Roberts

THE EVACUATION OF SINGAPORE

Stand By to Die, A.V. Sellwood
Surviving Tenko, the story of Margot Turner, Penny Starns
The Knights of Bushido, a short history of Japanese War Crimes, Lord Russell of Liverpool
The Shoe-horn Sonata, John Misto (prize-winning play)
The Will to Live, Sir John Smyth
Trove digitised newspapers, National Library of Australia
Unsung Heroes, Eleanor Nunis
Waiting for the Durian, Susan McCabe (story of internee Desmond Woodford)
We Too, Were There, Stories recalled by the Nursing Sisters of World War 2, Fedor Gould Fisher
While History Passed (first published as *In Japanese Hands*), Jessie Elizabeth Simons
White Coolies, Betty Jeffrey
Women Beyond the Wire, Lavinia Warner and John Sandilands

Diaries and memoirs of Jock Brodie, Shelagh Brown, Ellen Mavis Hannah, Horace Kendall, Murray Miller, Gordon Reis, Duncan Robertson, Harry Walker, drawing and doll made by Agnes (Betty) Jeffrey reproduced with her family's permission and Bill Bourke's father Lieutenant William Bourke's paintings, reproduced with Bill's permission.

And conversations with prisoners and their families, including many hours spent with my very dear friend, former internee Mr Neal Hobbs.

Neal Hobbs' birthday card.